COME OUT
FROM
AMONG
THEM

COME OUT FROM AMONG THEM

TODD COCONATO

CHARISMA HOUSE

Visit the author's website at PastorTodd.org, or visit charismahouse.com.

Cataloging-in-Publication Data is on file with the Library of Congress.
International Standard Book Number: 978-1-63641-259-7
E-book ISBN: 978-1-63641-260-3

2 2024
Printed in the United States of America

Most Charisma Media products are available at special quantity discounts for bulk purchase for sales promotions, premiums, fund-raising, and educational needs. For details, call us at (407) 333-0600 or visit our website at www. charismamedia.com.

CONTENTS

PREFACE

HAVE YOU EVER wondered why God put us on the earth at this specific time in history? After all, we could have been alive during a very different time—perhaps the time of the Roman Empire. Or we could have walked the earth during the days of Noah. We could have experienced the Great Depression, World War II, or even the Civil War. The truth is, there must be a reason why we are alive in this very hour, as I don't believe God made a mistake in bringing us into the world at this time in history.

God says clearly in His Word that He made us "fearfully and wonderfully" (Ps. 139:14). I believe it was for such a time as this! We are meant to represent Him as the *salt and the light*. The Bible says that faith without works is dead (Jas. 1:26). We are meant to be a people of action. These are essential facts we must consider as we think about our life's purpose in this critical hour. I believe this is a defining moment in history, and how we respond right now will have a significant impact on our children, their children, and generations to come, should the Lord tarry. It is truly a moment of decision.

God's intention for us as Christians, or followers of the Way, is to be His "body" here on earth. To be the head and not the tail (Deut. 28:13) and to influence the culture in a way that makes disciples of all nations, baptizing them in the name of the Father, Son, and Holy Spirit (Deut. 28:19–20). This is what the Bible refers to as the Great Commission. God intended that the culture be downstream of the church, yet for years it seems it has been the opposite, as much of the church has been swayed and influenced by the world. In many ways we have tried hard to look and act like the world and pop culture. It's apparent in most contemporary churches that Hollywood and society have greatly influenced much of what we see in the Christian culture of today—and that's a problem! We are called to be set apart. We are meant to be light in a dark place, not to look just like the world.

To put this all into perspective, God made us fearfully and wonderfully in His likeness and image, called us by name, and brought us into the world at this very moment in history for a reason! There is a reason, purpose, and significance for why you are the way you are, and I believe there is a calling on your life. This is why you have the convictions that you do in your heart. God has allowed you to experience the specific and unique experiences you have had to walk through—both good and bad—so that He can later use many of those same challenges and experiences for His glory. You have expertise in specific areas that no other human does, at least not in the exact same way that you do.

God often turns what was meant for evil around for good and shows His favor and blessing by restoring what the devil tried to kill, steal, and destroy by giving second and even third chances to those with enough faith and tenacity to press ahead and follow His ways. Repentance is also crucial in restoration and being right before God. Our testimony is formed when we do these things by His will and purposes, and His Holy Spirit anoints us as we do. Each of us has a testimony. The Bible says we shall overcome by the blood of the Lamb and by the word of our testimony. (See Revelation 12:11.) Our testimony is crucial to our walk, and we are told to speak it out.

God has given us promises of hope and a future (Jer. 29:11) and yes and amen (2 Cor. 1:20). He also said that He will be with us even until the end of the age (Matt. 28:20) and He will "never leave [us] nor forsake [us]" (Deut. 31:8). Furthermore He tells us it is the anointing that breaks the yoke of bondage (Isa. 10:27), and we are called to occupy until He comes (Luke 19:13). These promises are all very assuring and, if applied, give us all the confidence we need to know that the God of heaven and earth is on our side. Our identity in Jesus Christ means we are victorious. In other words, we are on the winning team! Do you operate that way? Do you know you are victorious as a child of the most high God?

I believe God has already placed a blueprint in the hearts of those willing to be like the prophet Isaiah and say the words, "Send me; I'll go." (See Isaiah 6:8.) The first step is our willingness to show up. When we show up, God will use us. He doesn't call the qualified but instead qualifies the called. The Lord responds to the prayers of the righteous and answers the call of salvation to those who call upon His name. Something happens in the spiritual realm when a believer exercises the faith to take a stand for righteousness. Just look at the many examples in God's Word where this is the case. God honors our obedience. He is a good Father!

Our heavenly Father empowers us with His Holy Spirit to fulfill our life's calling. He gives us all we will ever need to be successful in Him. He is more than enough. He is outside the constraints of time. Although we see through our finite human perspectives, God sees and knows everything. The Bible tells us He is "the Alpha and the Omega, the First and the Last, the Beginning and the End" (Rev. 22:13), and the great I Am.

Jesus was there at the beginning of all things and will also be there on the day of judgment. He is the Living Word. There is no other being that is equal to Him. Although we tend to fear Satan's attacks on our life, if we have decided to serve God, this automatically guarantees we cannot lose. It is written that as we persevere and press ahead, we will rule and reign with the Lord for all eternity. When we repent and turn from our wickedness, accept Jesus into our hearts as Lord and Savior, and decide to follow the ways of God, our names are written in the Lamb's Book of Life.

IT'S A FIXED FIGHT

The battle between good and evil is a fixed fight; God wins every time. Although there may be times when it doesn't look like we will win, as believers in Jesus Christ we are ultimately set up for success both in this world and for all eternity. We can rest assured in this truth. The apostle Paul said that "to live is Christ and to die is gain" (Phil. 1:21). Ultimately we are just passing through this world, called to be in it but not of it.

It is imperative that we embrace and understand the full potential of what is available to us as believers. Many Christians fail to realize what we have at our disposal when we muster up the courage, faith, and strength to walk forward in the calling of God on our lives and put on the whole armor of God!

WE ARE SET UP FOR SUCCESS

As Christians we have the answer for all the problems of this life. God gave us every tool we will ever need to live abundant and thriving lives no matter what happens in the world around us. We have the solution for this broken world: *Jesus is the answer.* God laid everything out for us in the BIBLE: Basic Instructions Before Leaving Earth. It's similar to being in high school and somehow having the answer key to each test and exam.

God has also given believers His Holy Spirit, which gives us the power and authority to pull down strongholds, walk in God's anointing, heal the sick, receive wisdom and discernment from above, and persevere through every trial and test. According to the Bible, we can cast out demons and drive them out of territories, and we can set the captives free from any ailment, sickness, or disease. Scripture tells us we can perform the same miracles that Christ did throughout His earthly ministry, and even greater things! (See John 14:12.) Think about how significant this all is. We can be history makers, movers and shakers, and change the situation in every challenge that comes our way as we move forward in our faith.

THE PROBLEM

The church and believers worldwide have fallen into a state of apathy and complacency over the last few decades. For the most part, the Western church fell asleep and allowed the culture to dictate what we should do and how we should operate. We became distracted and allowed doubt, fear, and the pressure from the modern cancel-culture mentality to pressure us into a state of slumber and cause us to back down on many important, nonnegotiable areas and issues of our faith and beliefs. As a result, much of the church is walking out an almost powerless form of Christianity. It is like what the Bible addresses in the Book of Revelation as the "compromised church" or the churches of Sardis and Laodicea—having a form of godliness but denying the power thereof. It's a tainted version of Christianity filled with compromise and "leaven." This is why so much of our world has fallen off the cliff into the morally bankrupt abyss and the very egregious situation we are seeing play out all around us. The Bible says God will spit out (Rev. 3:16) the lukewarm and warns that "a little leaven leavens the whole lump" (Gal. 5:9, NKJV).

THE GOOD NEWS

The good news is that there is a remnant. And whenever there is a remnant, God is not done moving. The remnant is made up of those who are willing to stand in faith and believe in the promises of God. The remnant comprises those of us ready to show up and answer the call of God on our lives in this critical hour. We walk in the anointing of the Holy Spirit. We are not fearful; we know that God is with us. We also understand our authority in Jesus Christ and walk in that authority. We have the faith needed to please God and walk in His favor.

The remnant is bold and not compromised or given to the enticement and temptations of the enemy around us. We do not worship idols or succumb to the pressure of disconnecting from the entirety of the Word of God and its teaching and instruction. We are willing to stand and trust God in all circumstances. We are set apart and strive to live in a consecrated manner. When the times get tough, we press ahead and endure, knowing God is with us even in our valley experiences.

We do not lose hope or allow the world to get us down. We know that we are on the winning team and walk in that confidence. We are focused on the mission!

A remnant person wakes up every day and asks the Lord, "What can I do to please You and be about Your business this day?" It's not about us or what we want; instead we inquire of God as to what He wants us to do. We pray God's will and submit ourselves to His will for our lives. In other words, we don't do things for our recognition or our glory but rather for His glory. It's not about us; it's all about Him.

The remnant's mission is the Great Commission—souls. To know God and to make Him known in the world. We always live in view of eternity, yet we strive to be salt and light here on earth as representatives of the King of kings and Lord of lords. He is our One and only God; there are no other gods in our lives. A remnant believer regularly spends time in the secret place and has an active prayer life. We also are worshippers and good repenters.

In the very challenging environment in which we find ourselves as a nation and world, the remnant must lead and rise to the many tasks at hand. When I refer to the remnant, I mean those willing to believe and live out the entirety of God's Word, those who hunger and thirst for righteousness!

In this book we will lay out a strategy from heaven for believers to "come out from among them" (2 Cor.

6:17, KJV) and answer the call of God on our lives in this critical hour. As I mentioned, we were made for such a time as this—the fact that you are alive now is no mistake. We must answer the call of God, take our position, and stand! We will discuss this in detail in the chapters ahead. God laid out in His Word a strategy and path forward for His body. It's time for the people of God to lead this culture and take back the territory for the kingdom of God. This is precisely what we will do. So, let's begin!

CHAPTER 1

THE RISING REMNANT AND WHERE WE CAME FROM

O VER THE PAST several years, our world has experienced a noticeable shift. Have you seen it? We are truly living in extraordinary times! Many people yearn to return to "normal," but I believe we will not see what many consider to be normal again. That is a good thing, however, as we could not have continued in the direction in which we were headed. We have advanced into a new era and season. The hour is rapidly getting late, and we are seeing biblical prophecy play out before our eyes.

The Bible says you can't put new wine into old wineskins (Matt. 9:16–17; Mark 2:22; Luke 5:33–39). We are certainly in a "new wineskin" season. Even though many concerning things are taking place, I believe this is an exciting hour for the church. This is what we trained for. *This is meant to be the church's greatest hour and our time to shine.* We can—and I believe we will—witness a great end-time harvest before the Lord returns! The revival has already begun, and it will accelerate. Be ready. It will be the best of times and the worst of times at the same time.

From wars and rumors of the war raging around the globe to cycles of civil unrest playing out in many countries to wicked and godless leaders running much of the world, there is an urgency in the hearts of those who have ears to hear and eyes to see all that is taking place. I believe God has called many of us to be watchmen on the wall and sound the alarm as voices in the wilderness. I often refer to it as an Issachar anointing of understanding and discerning the times. If you feel this urgency in your heart, you are not alone. This has caused many remnant believers to endure difficult situations such as being ostracized and estranged from family and friends, accused, shamed, publicly maligned, and forced into engaging in a real battle of good versus evil. No true believer can avoid engaging in this battle; if you are filled with the Holy Spirit, you will be drawn into it.

This has all spilled over into our jobs and workplaces, the companies we patronize, our family and friend circles, the government, schools and universities, and even large parts of the church. This is not a time when believers can stay in the "mushy middle," as God has allowed the environment around us to become so polarized that we must take a side, be bold, and stand. When we do this, battles will arise that we must fight to stand for our faith in this hour. It's not easy, but it is necessary. Many people I know, including myself, have paid a high cost for standing. If you are standing, you understand what I mean. Thank you for standing for the truth. The Bible says, "Let us not grow weary in doing good" (Gal. 6:9, MEV). However, sometimes that's easier said than done.

A SEASON OF CHANGE

Change is all around us, from the educational institutions that are essentially brainwashing our young people and working as indoctrination camps for our kids to the moral depravity we see in movies and television and on our streaming devices and platforms. More men and women are addicted to pornography than ever before, as the devil has made every sin imaginable instantly available and at our fingertips. Addictions are running rampant, as many families have to deal with one or more loved ones who are addicted to drugs and alcohol or some illicit substance or pharmaceutical/prescription drug. There are many other addictions as well. I deal with this issue daily as I counsel people. Many people are highly stressed, depressed, and overwhelmed by their situation. The church is not doing well in addressing these matters; they are often swept under the rug rather than being dealt with, further complicating the case for the individuals involved.

Many teens are cutting themselves, withdrawing from family, living in rebellion, and/or becoming sexually active at a very early age. They are also more prone to engage in same-sex attraction, have identity confusion, and dabble with multiple sexual partners simultaneously as "alternative lifestyles" are being pushed by the government, schools, celebrities, influencers, and the media. This has dramatically advanced even since the early 2000s. Parents must be more vigilant than ever.

Sexual promiscuity and perversion are at an all-time high as many lack the self-value and self-worth to resist the temptation of giving their bodies to sex outside of marriage or to depraved sexual acts. It is also not being effectively countered from the pulpit as many preachers fear speaking on issues deemed controversial, so they skirt around and stay silent on key areas for fear of reprisal. This is especially the case in many mega-churches that have grown so fast and so large that they are often handcuffed by their seeker-friendly church growth models, congregants, and boards to not speak on anything that could ruffle the feathers of their donors and many lukewarm attendees. We will discuss this later.

THE DESTRUCTION OF THE FAMILY UNIT

We also see the family unit being ripped apart by our institutional hierarchy, cancel culture, leftism, and the introduction of what former president Obama referred to as new social norms. More and more marriages are failing around us, even in the church—another casualty of the world's system.

To be clear, I am not here to attack or condemn you if

you have had multiple marriages or even one divorce. If anything, I yearn to see you walking into a new season of God's promises and plans for your life. I, too, have a past from which I've had to seek God for healing and restoration. We can't change what has happened, but we can learn from it and not repeat it. We must speak to such things and identify our challenges as the body of Christ.

My leadership philosophy is to first identify the challenges and issues before finding real, tangible, biblical solutions to each problem. Please remember that once you have repented and walked away from repetitive sin, it is in the sea of forgetfulness according to the Word of the Lord: "There is now no condemnation for those who are in Christ Jesus" (Rom. 8:1). The key is that we must be teachable, accountable, and willing to learn from our mistakes. When I was younger in the faith a mentor told me, "A smart man learns from his own mistakes, but a wise man learns from the mistakes of others." That is true. God wants us to walk in the conviction of His Holy Spirit and be willing to course-correct when we make a mistake.

Everyone makes mistakes at times. The key is that we get back up and keep pressing ahead! We lose only when we give up. One of the big problems in the church is that people put pastors and other ministry leaders on a pedestal and think they don't make mistakes, so when a leader fails or does something wrong, it's more disruptive. In many cases these leaders make things worse by doubling down in pride rather than exercising humility, acknowledging the severity of the situation, and admitting their guilt.

As the body of Christ moves forward, I pray that more pastors and ministry leaders will be transparent about their humanity rather than trying to uphold the mirage that they are perfect. I often speak about how I am far from perfect and simply a messenger preaching and teaching God's Word. I do, however, make a solid effort to avoid even the appearance of evil (1 Thess. 5:22) and to be a good testimony to others who are watching.

If you are a leader, remember you will be judged to a higher standard. I have a healthy fear of the Lord, and I think it's vital that we all do. It's a good fear, and a necessary one, kind of like when we were children and feared getting spanked by Dad or Mom. In most cases Dad and Mom were looking out for our best interests and loved us enough to reprimand us. The Bible says, "Whoever spares the rod hates their children" (Prov. 13:24), which is where we get the saying "Spare the rod, spoil the child." Discipline is part of love. We must bring this back into our parenting, or our children will not be set up to succeed when they are adults. A good fear of the Lord keeps us in check spiritually. We should all fear the Lord.

When good leaders make mistakes, they are willing to course-correct and shift their oversights into teachable moments. They show how to fix the problem honestly rather than deny that anything wrong happened.

A major issue we are facing in the body of Christ is that few people want to confront sin these days. We also see a lot of things swept under the rug. This has done tremendous damage, as sin or corruption must be addressed in love and dealt with properly.

In defense of pastors and ministry leaders, I will say that people can be vicious and lack mercy when a spiritual leader does happen to fall. It's equally important that we all seek understanding and come to the aid of those of our brethren who fall or have something tragic happen in the ministry. We can't kick each other when we are down. The body of Christ is meant to rally around our wounded and lovingly help them back to restoration. We are good at pointing fingers but not so good at being the hands and arms of Christ. Certainly we can all do better in this regard.

Many people have to deal with tragic or challenging situations without the support of the local church. Some leaders need more time to offer help because they are focused on church growth strategies. The seeker-friendly, microwave version of Christianity that has dominated Western culture has caused the church to evolve into something quite different from what it was only a few decades ago. The church also has a real issue with what I call "celebrity Christianity," in which large ministries and their leadership live and act as though they are Hollywood celebrities, losing touch with their original mission or congregation and humble beginnings.

God honors the humble and contrite. His Word says, "Humble yourselves in the sight of the Lord, and He will lift you up" (Jas. 4:10, NKJV). Unless the Lord builds the house, we labor in vain. (See Psalm 127:1.) I believe the church has raised up many people who have talent but lack the anointing of the Holy Spirit. Skill and talent are much different from anointing. You can't fake the anointing. This is a big problem as unless God truly anoints a person, he or she will eventually fail and cause significant collateral damage in his or her failure.

MANY ARE HURT AND WOUNDED BY THE CHURCH

I don't entirely fault those of you who had to deal with a problematic area and were not given the needed pastoral care or discipleship while you were under spiritual attack. This lack of help probably caused the problem to get much worse than it needed to. This happened to me as well, so I understand. As a pastor, I want to repent for the lack of shepherds in the body of Christ. Praise God, there are many real shepherds; however, while others have been focused on their followings, fortunes, and building their kingdoms rather than God's kingdom, many of you were victims of these things and couldn't find someone willing to help you in your time of need. That gives me a righteous anger, as it was never God's intention!

I can't tell you how many people I meet all over the

country who tell me they either don't know their pastor or they can't get in to speak with one, no matter how hard they tried. Has this been your experience as well? I believe this is why we must have a personal relationship with God and not rely on a person to be the conduit between God and us. We pastors must help to foster a stronger relationship between the individuals in our churches and God.

ACCOUNTABILITY AND MENTORSHIP

As the body of Christ walked away from mentorship, discipleship, and accountability, we opened a massive door for the enemy to have a field day in the lives of newer and ill-equipped believers. Even some veterans in the faith were hit with a barrage from the enemy and were left to fend for themselves. Again, we as a body must do better in these areas as well. This is one reason God had me write this book.

I have tremendous mercy for those who have legitimately been hurt in the church. How can we expect someone who hears only one or two scriptures a week and gets a motivational and extreme grace–type message from their pastor to be set up for true success when the storms of life come? It's simple: we can't! This is a significant issue and a major reason why we are where we are.

We are even witnessing entire denominations essentially rewriting fundamental core Christian doctrines such as the definitions of marriage and gender. "Wokeism" and compromise have become cancers throughout the global body of Christ. The old-time Pentecostal evangelists and preachers of the early and mid-twentieth century have almost vanished in many places. They have been replaced with men who have lost their masculinity and women who have had to step up in critical areas where fathers and husbands have recanted and are, in many cases, neglecting their obligation to lead their families in a Christlike and biblical manner and to love their wives "as Christ loved the church" (Eph. 5:25).

There is a way forward, a healthy way forward, which we will discuss later.

THE RISE OF THE REMNANT

Sir Isaac Newton's third law of motion tells us every action has an equal and opposite reaction, so while all the above was happening, something else happened simultaneously. While COVID-19 and other related developments have rocked our world and significantly disrupted our lives, these things have led to a perfect storm allowing a group of people I refer to as "the remnant" to arise.

I believe that what is referred to as the mainstream church has separated itself in many ways from doctrinally sound biblical Christianity. In contrast, a group of people who walk in discernment and the conviction of the Holy Spirit have had enough of this watered-down teaching and have risen up. These same people know the answer will not be found in a politician or even through science or education; the people of God must take back this nation and world by returning to the fundamentals of our faith. We must restore the foundations. It's time to go back to the basics!

During the Trump era, many looked to President Trump to fight the battles of the church—which in some cases he did—but ultimately he couldn't save us. Some people have built whole ministries based on Trump's return. While I support him, we must shift the focus back to Jesus and not make it about any man. Trump is simply a man whom God used for a specific purpose, much like He did with King Cyrus and others throughout the Bible.

While that story may not be over just yet, the people of God must now be the ones to stand up according to what I like to call the Bible's recipe for revival, found in 2 Chronicles 7:14: "If *my* people..." (emphasis added). God wants *His people* to stand up and repent and turn back to Him. He wants us to call upon His name and contend, fast, and pray for our nation and culture. The spotlight is now on the church. This is why God has allowed this time. I don't believe either our nation or the world is done, but we must act now. America is meant to be a Nineveh, not a Sodom and Gomorrah. This is why repentance must be the message; it leads to revival and new life in Jesus Christ.

THE END IS NOT YET!

When the war in Ukraine started boiling up and many were fearful that it could go nuclear, I heard people saying it could be the end. I went to the Lord in prayer and fasting and asked if we were entering the tribulation period, and God assured me that we would see "one more round" and the end is not yet. That is when I realized this remnant that we see rising was called for such a time as this and God is cleaning up His bride, the church. This is what is happening right now. In this season, God is preparing His church for His return and for what is to come. It is our moment to shine. This is what we have trained for.

Those who have taken a bold stance and stood firm in this time have seen miraculous things in their lives and ministries. Many remnant pastors and leaders are experiencing exponential growth in their churches and in the number of people who follow them and look to their leadership. I have seen this play out at our ministry as we have seen many doors open and experienced extreme growth in the last few years. I believe God will put His favor and anointing on anyone willing to make souls their mission and who is about the business of the Lord. If we stand for the entirety of God's Word, His hand of favor and blessing will be upon us.

When the children of Israel went into rebellion and started to worship idols, God sent His (real) prophets to warn them that they would see punishment and the wrath of God for their disobedience and sin. Several times God allowed them to go into captivity, where they eventually would return to the roots of their faith and once again worship the God of Abraham, Isaac, and Jacob. When they did repent and turn back to God, He eventually freed them from their captors and allowed them to be restored as a nation and a people.

God would have to apologize to Israel if He did not hold us to a similar standard as a nation and church. In His Word, God is clear that He will come back for a church without "spot or wrinkle" (Eph. 5:27, NKJV). It certainly appears that God is refining His church and course-correcting us so we may get back into His will. I believe God has extended His mercy in this season so we can return to Him. It is a pivotal crossroads period. The time is short for the people of God to respond. What will we do?

WHO WERE THE PROPHETS IN THE BIBLE?

The role of the prophets in the Bible is significant, as they played a critical part in the history of Israel and the development of Judaism and Christianity. Prophets are people who have received direct communication from God, and their messages are intended to convey God's will to the people.

The role of the prophets began in the Old Testament, with the earliest prophets being figures such as Abraham, Moses, and Samuel. These figures were not formally called prophets, but they played a similar role in communicating God's will to the people. The first prophet explicitly referred to as such in the Bible was Isaiah, who lived in the eighth century BC.

The primary role of the prophets was to serve as intermediaries between God and the people. They were tasked with communicating God's messages to the people and warning them of the consequences of disobedience. The prophets were often critical of the ruling authorities and the religious leaders of their time, and their messages were often unpopular with the people.

The prophets were also responsible for the development of the concept of monotheism in Judaism. Before the prophets, the Jewish people believed in multiple gods, but the prophets emphasized the importance of worshipping only one God. The prophet Elijah famously challenged the prophets of Baal, a Canaanite god, and demonstrated the power of the one true God.

In addition to their role as messengers, the prophets also played a significant role in shaping the religious practices and traditions of the Jewish people. They were responsible for establishing the importance of prayer, fasting, and almsgiving, and they played a critical role in the development of the synagogue as a place of worship.

The prophecies of the Old Testament are also significant for Christians, as they predicted the coming of Jesus. Many of the Old Testament prophecies described a coming Messiah who would save the Jewish people, and Christians believe that Jesus was this promised Messiah.

In the New Testament, the role of the prophets was somewhat different. The apostles were often described as prophets, and they played a critical role in spreading the message of Jesus to the world. The Book of Revelation, written by the apostle John, is often referred to as a prophetic work because it contains visions of the end of the world and the return of Jesus.

The role of the prophets in the Bible was significant, as they played a critical part in the history of Israel and the development of Judaism and Christianity. Their messages of hope, warning, and redemption continue to inspire people around the world, and their influence can still be felt in the religious practices and traditions of many cultures.

ADDRESSING FALSE PROPHECY

Whenever a public figure, especially a modern preacher, even slightly indicates something about his stance on a hot-button issue, many people will automatically rush to judgment, put words in his mouth, or assume something untrue.

People often tell me, "Pastor, you don't need to explain yourself." I understand, and I agree for the most part. However, they don't see the hundreds of emails and all the communication we get each week from people in real need or challenging situations. They are not in my shoes. When I repeatedly see the same question or series of questions, I realize there is confusion about an issue. Chaos often breeds contention or even worse, as people often see things from their perspective and through their own experiences. Confusion has started unnecessary wars.

My heart is for God and for you. I take my role as a shepherd very seriously. That is why I address things and have the needed conversations even when they are challenging to navigate. My philosophy is that there is always a path forward. No matter how challenging it may look, there is a way that we can inquire of the Lord, get His strategy, and move forward in victory as people of God.

Biblically, leaders are held to a higher standard. One of the most challenging things about my role is taking a stand that goes against the narrative or current popular opinion. I receive all kinds of responses, both friendly and not-so-friendly. However, I must obey God.

> Little children, keep yourselves from idols.
> —1 JOHN 5:21, NKJV

I want to be very clear about where I see challenges in the church right now and why, in my opinion, it's essential we course-correct here from a biblical standpoint.

1. Idolatry. The Bible is clear that we are not to have or make idols of man. There is only one God. As humans we are prone to making idols. We saw this repeatedly in ancient Israel, and it is still prevalent today. It can be a real trap to newer believers or those not in tune with what the Bible says.

Over the last few years, I have seen many people making idols of man in the prophetic community. It's almost like the followers of the Grateful Dead. These people can be very loyal and follow some of these folks anywhere, often not taking their stances and teachings to the Lord. There is a contingent of people who follow some of these internet "prophets" from event to event and lean on their every word as if their words were the Bible. That is dangerous, as their words are *not* equivalent to the Bible. People also do this with pastors, by the way, and others. It's all wrong. Any faithful pastor, preacher, or prophet should lead his or her followers to God and His Word toward a healthy and balanced Christian lifestyle, not act as a Christian celebrity or as if he or she is the sole person who can hear from God for everyone else.

I believe in prophecy and think there are real prophets. I am friends with many prophets. But my advice is to test the spirits and make sure that what is being said bears witness in your heart and aligns with the Word of God. This is key. Make sure that you don't make an idol out of any person. There shall be no other gods before our one and only true God!

2. My sheep hear My voice. The Bible is clear that believers can listen to the voice of the Lord for themselves. While hearing from true prophets is essential, it's also crucial that we have our own prayer life and can understand and recognize the voice of the Lord speaking to us. The Holy Spirit gives us wisdom and discernment in our daily faith walk. We all need insight, especially at this late hour. I often talk about how we are navigating through a spiritual minefield right now. All church leaders should teach their followers to hear from the Lord for themselves.

Again, newer believers are prone to being abused in this area as they often have less confidence about hearing for themselves. The Bible says, "In the mouth of two or three witnesses shall every word be established" (2 Cor. 13:1, MEV). This is very important. Confirmation helps when we are unsure if something is of the Lord. We shouldn't look to just one person to tell us what God wants to speak to us. God set up a system of checks and balances around us, and with that agreement and confirmation we can feel much more confident that a word is in fact from God.

3. Prophecy on demand. Many people are seeking a new word. While this is good, the previous two points must be applied in this process. People often ask me for a word or comment, and I can only give them what God gives me! I can't make something up to please them. Sometimes I get a word for the person in that moment, but often I don't. We must always be accurate and authentic and avoid the temptation to speak from our flesh. Speaking from the flesh is very dangerous, as people hang on to these words and make huge life decisions based on them. Most comments from God come from a place of good and healthy fear and trembling, a fear that you know is from God.

What an honor that God uses prophetic voices to speak His heart! When a prophetic voice receives a word, they deliver it in obedience to God. A true prophetic word will never go against the Bible. It will also not change the Bible. If either of those things happens, it's a wrong word. As I mentioned above, it should also bear witness in your heart, as you, a believer in Christ, are filled with the Holy Spirit. Always ask the Holy Spirit, "Is this You?" When we ask, He will answer.

4. Be mindful of false narratives. Many Christians believe that the "Q" movement is accurate, Donald Trump is currently the president, and the military is now running our country. This is not happening. Trust me. If I'm wrong, I will not only repent to you all, but I will be rejoicing with you. But as I have investigated extensively and prayed long and hard about this, I don't believe these things are true.

Here is the challenge: many prophetic words sound almost identical to Q. Be cautious! The message can be rebranded and repacked as a "prophecy." As the body of Christ, we must be wise and understand that our credibility is on the line here. The world is watching. We can't fall into the enemy's trap designed to discredit the church. We must stick to the primary mission and not get pulled into distractions set up to cause us to look foolish.

5. Don't touch My anointed. Many people quote the scripture, "Touch not my anointed ones" (Ps. 105:15, ESV). The Bible is true, and I believe in this scripture. However, we can't use this as an excuse to not correct false statements and doctrine. It grieves my heart to see some prominent individuals known as prophets say bizarre and unbiblical things in the name of prophecy. Please ask yourselves if what these people are saying is from God. Roller coasters in heaven? Jell-O mountains? Again, we must remember the world is watching us. Let's stick to whatever is pure, holy, and scriptural! Otherwise, we lose credibility.

I am not against any one person. I love people. I am also not questioning anyone's salvation; that is up to God. We can look for a person's fruit and ask the Holy Spirit for wisdom and guidance on who is honest. My motive is the protection of the saints and the church's credibility. We need to make some changes. We need to stop making idols and emphasizing specific gifts more than needed and get back to our primary mission—souls! Let's operate in doctrinally sound, biblical Christianity.

HOW WE CAN COURSE-CORRECT

Anyone who has gained significant influence or followers must take that responsibility very seriously and be faithful to our calling and God's Word. We can't be pulled into saying things that are untrue to appease our audience or following. We can't become focused on money or fame in any way; they will not last, as God gives and takes away. We must fear God and be about His business. It is *His* ministry, not ours! This isn't a time to attack one another or engage in back-and-forth slandering.

God is using our current situation to purify His bride and get us planted on a firm foundation—Jesus Christ and His Word! We need to be focused on the Great Commission. The enemy would much rather us be about the Great Division! Be mindful of this. I felt the need to address this here, as God has put it on my heart heavily in recent months. I rarely feel the need to speak so bluntly, but we must get away from the weirdness and get back to the Word and truth. Again, I believe in prophecy, and I am not against any particular person. All I can do is provide the facts according to the Word of God, and each individual must take this to the Lord themselves and receive revelation from the Holy Spirit.

If you are a prophet and you are reading this, I am not against you. I have many dear friends who are prophets whom I love and respect. I am not questioning your sincerity but rather taking my advice and ensuring I align with God's Word, as I have written above. I have made mistakes over the years and am thankful for accountability and transparency, for people who loved me and cared enough about me to share the truth so I could make the needed changes and get into God's perfect will. We don't want to see your ministry discredited or hurt in any way. We love you. I love you. God loves you. It's especially essential in this internet age that we listen to sound voices and those who hold themselves accountable, not to lone rangers and people who are untethered from the more excellent body of Christ.

This is a season of much-needed course correction. As the dust settles, we will be set up for success and on the level where we need to be. This has happened in the past, and the adults in the room had to issue a rebuke and speak in God's love to the areas of imbalance to help the church get back on track. We all must be teachable and willing to take these crucial matters to the Lord.

IS IT BIBLICAL TO CALL OUT FALSE DOCTRINE AND PROPHECY?

Is it scriptural for someone to call out a false prophecy or incorrect doctrine according to the Word of God? This is something I am often asked as a pastor. Many people are afraid to say anything about this subject for concern that they may open a can of worms or for fear of reprisal. However, the Bible tells us we are to judge a prophetic word as well as the actions and fruit of other believers.

Paul wrote, "Let two or three prophets speak, and let the others pass judgment" (1 Cor. 14:29, NASB). Notice that according to Scripture, the prophetic word is to be judged. Nowhere does the Bible say we shouldn't judge prophetic words or any teachings that are incorrect.

Paul also wrote:

> But even if we, or an angel from heaven, should preach to you a gospel contrary to what we have preached to you, he is to be accursed!
>
> —GALATIANS 1:8, NASB

> For what have I to do with judging outsiders? Is it not those inside the church whom you are to judge? God judges those outside. "Purge the evil person from among you."
>
> —1 CORINTHIANS 5:12–13, ESV

> But now I am writing to you not to associate with anyone who bears the name of brother if he is guilty of sexual immorality or greed, or is an idolater, reviler, drunkard, or swindler—not even to eat with such a one.
>
> —1 CORINTHIANS 5:11, ESV

Many Christians tend to do the opposite of what Scripture is saying here. Often we judge the nonbeliever but are afraid to judge the believer's fruit and actions. Yet Scripture is pretty clear that we are meant to judge the believer's fruit and actions and leave judgment of the nonbeliever up to God. It's a common misconception, and I have even heard other preachers say we should not judge other Christians. The Book of Hebrews says, "For the word of God is living and active, sharper than any two-edged sword, piercing to the division of soul and of spirit, of joints and of marrow, and discerning the thoughts and intentions of the heart. And no creature is hidden from his sight, but all are naked and exposed to the eyes of him to whom we must give account" (Heb. 4:12–13, ESV).

We believers need to be careful about this because when we withhold loving correction, we do a disservice to those who desire to be right before God but have not yet been discipled or mentored enough to know they are in error. A godly correction from an elder or mentor is actually a display of God's love, as it sets us up for success by allowing us to make the necessary course correction and get back into God's will for our lives. I can't even tell you how many times over the years an elder or mentor in my life has corrected me and helped me. This is a system of checks and balances that God designed to keep us healthy and protected. So, the answer is simple. Are Christians to judge others in the church? Yes.

According to Dr. Christopher Cone, "Christians are supposed to hold each other accountable for our actions" in love. Sin should also be confronted. Still, it is not our job to judge "someone else's position (whether they are actually a believer or not) if they are claiming to be a brother or sister in Christ, nor are we to judge those outside the church, as God instructs us not to.[1] It's important to understand the distinction.

I'm not telling you to become a heresy hunter or to make this your focus. Many continually look to judge others and even make this their ministry, which creates an unhealthy balance in their focus and attention.

Walking in God's love, grace, and mercy is essential. We must have compassion and grace. God wants us to focus on what is pure, holy, and righteous and to be about His business. But according to Scripture, there is also a time for judgment given in love within the church.

RED MEAT CHRISTIANITY

Many people are looking for an exotic version of Christianity, following whatever the latest "it" thing is in the church. It is like red meat. This hurts people because the focus is not on the Bible but on the idea of having some type of new, secret knowledge or inside information.

Here is the problem: If the gospel message is boring and you seek something exotic, what you find will be no different from other incorrect teachings and even false religions. Jesus is the same yesterday, today, and forever (Heb. 13:8). Our life in Christ will not be sustainable unless we build our house on a firm foundation. His Word is also the same yesterday, today, and forever; it was there in the beginning. No one is to change or usurp the Word of God.

Seeking an exotic version of Christianity is a red flag, as these ministries are sustained by someone's personality and the latest thing they said or came up with rather than the Word of God. Followers of these ministries are led to depend on a person rather than hear from God for themselves.

Many arguments have started over this concept because people don't want their party to be rained on, but if you want to endure until the end, the key is to get back to the Bible, souls, and kingdom business. Study to show yourself approved (2 Tim. 2:15)!

Faith comes from hearing, and hearing by the Word of God (Rom. 10:17). There is no biblical argument for this red meat version of Christianity. That's why people have to make up excuses and reflect and deflect when it's confronted.

Look, God didn't spare my life from nine stab wounds so that I could lie to you. I love you enough to tell you the truth. And by the way, I'm far from perfect. But that doesn't mean I will simply give in and go along with anything. You can take it or leave it, but I will not be pressured into lying to you or promoting ideas that oppose biblical Christianity.

I could quickly point out many of these wrong ideas. I could make a series of videos breaking them down and lay out facts with Scripture. But for now I am simply warning the saints that we need to course-correct and get back to the Lord's business.

CHAPTER 2

SEPARATING FROM BABYLON AND THE SYSTEM

THE CHURCH PLAYS a vital role in society. It sets the moral tone and helps keep people from walking into spiritual darkness that affects all areas of their lives, including their households and families. When there is a lack of church leadership or the government tries to play the church's role and people accept it, the result is what we see all around us today—moral depravity, lawlessness, corruption, and wickedness in the land. That is because the moral compass has been altered or broken. We have seen this happen repeatedly throughout history, including in ancient Israel. When a nation moves away from God, these things always manifest in some form.

It is the obligation and rightful duty of church leaders and believers alike to speak to such matters of wickedness and expose the lies and propaganda being pushed on the people by an out-of-control state. Fake news, disinformation, social conditioning, and more are coming at us from all angles. We must protect people from being deceived as best we can and not willingly go along with false information.

Think of Shadrach, Meshach, and Abednego. (See

Daniel 3.) God required them to take a very uncomfortable stand by not bowing down to idols. While their stance had a high cost, landing them in a fiery furnace, another One was with them in the fire. Their lives were spared, and they were given great favor for taking a very tough stand! Suppose more people spoke out, and the others were held accountable to biblical principles—think of how this would change the current environment! Truth and morality would be upheld, the rule of law would again be established, and society could return to a healthy state. The governmental leadership (or lack thereof) is almost always a reflection of a society's spiritual condition. I say culture is downstream of the church.

We can't sit on the sidelines and watch what's happening around us, expecting someone else to rescue us. We must use this time to equip the people and call our nation back to God. He is ultimately our only hope, yet He is all the hope we could ever need and more than enough! Otherwise, if we maintain our current trajectory, we will continue to lose freedoms, and the very egregious things we are witnessing will escalate. Unless the moral compass is fixed and set back to biblical morality, values, truth, and common sense, this decline can only accelerate, and we will continue to follow the momentum and head off into the moral abyss.

This is a critical moment for our nation and the world, and taking wise action is the solution. We need a revival. If we answer complacency with more complacency and apathy with more apathy, we will not get the desired result of a change in the right direction. God laid out the recipe for revival very clearly in His Word. He told us in 2 Chronicles what we must do to regain His blessing and favor, which will heal our land:

> If my people, who are called by my name, will humble themselves and pray and seek my face and turn from their wicked ways, then I will hear from heaven, and I will forgive their sin and will heal their land.
>
> —2 Chronicles 7:14

How do things change? When people take action. Applied biblical wisdom combined with divine strategy is the answer. The church is meant to lead in all areas of society. We can change the situation—it's called the Great Commission!

ANCIENT BABYLON AND WHAT WE NEED TO KNOW

The Babylonian captivity is the period in Israel's history when the Jews were taken captive by King Nebuchadnezzar II of Babylon. This shows us not only the fulfillment of biblical prophecy but also how the people of ancient Israel went off course, ended up in exile, and were later restored once they repented and turned back to God.

God used Babylon to bring judgment on Israel for the people's idolatry and rebellion several times. Throughout Scripture we see the clear battle of light versus darkness and how when the Israelites fell into idolatry and out of alignment with God, they would find themselves captive by a foreign army. These stories are depicted in the Old Testament account and still have significance for us today.

According to Got Questions ministries, "With each rebellion against Babylonian rule, Nebuchadnezzar would lead his armies against Judah until they laid siege to Jerusalem for over a year, killing many people and destroying the Jewish temple, taking captive many thousands of Jews, and leaving Jerusalem in ruins.

"As prophesied in Scripture, the Jewish people would be allowed to return to Jerusalem after seventy years of exile. That prophecy was fulfilled in 537 BC, and the Jews were allowed by King Cyrus of Persia to return to Israel."[1]

REVIVAL IN ISRAEL AND THEN BACK TO CAPTIVITY

The people's return to Israel under the direction of Ezra led to a revival among the Jewish people and the rebuilding of the temple.[2] Note that each time there was a restoration period, it was in alignment with what God suggested in 2 Chronicles 7:14. God is not a man that He should lie. He stands by His Word, the ultimate truth, which is the same yesterday, today, and forever. This is why we are looking into these events, as there is nothing new under the sun.

Nebuchadnezzar II was the king of the Neo-Babylonian Empire, which existed from 626 BC to 539 BC. During his reign, which began in 605 BC, the Babylonian army conquered Jerusalem, which was the capital of the kingdom of Judah, and took many Jews into captivity.

The Babylonian captivity, also known as the Babylonian exile, lasted for seventy years and was a significant event in Jewish history. Nebuchadnezzar's conquest of Judah and Jerusalem led to the destruction of the first temple and the exile of the Jewish people to Babylon.

During this captivity the Jews were forced to live in Babylon, where they were subjected to cultural and religious assimilation. However, despite the challenges they faced, the Jewish community managed to maintain their identity and culture through their religious practices, traditions, and Scripture.

This period of captivity marked a significant period of Jewish history and had a profound impact on Jewish culture and identity. The events of this time are recorded in the Hebrew Bible, and the story of the Jewish people's exile and return to Jerusalem is commemorated annually in the Jewish holiday of Passover.

The Jews experienced a significant revival during the time of Ezra, which occurred after their return from Babylonian exile. Ezra, who was a priest and scribe, played a pivotal role in this revival.

When the Jews returned to Jerusalem, they found the city and the temple in ruins. Ezra, with the help of Nehemiah, led the people in the task of rebuilding the temple and the city walls. This physical rebuilding helped to renew the people's sense of national and religious identity.

Ezra also initiated a spiritual revival by teaching and interpreting the Law of Moses to the people. He organized public readings of the Law, which helped the people to understand its meaning and significance. He also worked to reform the people's religious practices and eradicate pagan influences that had crept into their worship.

One of the most significant moments of the revival occurred when the people gathered in Jerusalem to celebrate the Feast of Tabernacles. During the celebration, Ezra read the Law aloud to the people, and they responded with weeping and repentance. This event marked a turning point in the spiritual life of the people and led to their renewed commitment to follow God's commands.

The return of the Israelites from Babylonian captivity marked a significant period in Jewish history. After being exiled to Babylon for seventy years, the Israelites were allowed to return to their homeland by the Persian king Cyrus the Great. The period following their return was characterized by a renewed emphasis on the worship of God, as the Israelites sought to rebuild their temple and reestablish their religious practices.

IDOLATRY

One of the key lessons the Israelites learned from their exile was the danger of idolatry. Before the exile many Israelites had fallen into the worship of false gods, which led to their downfall and captivity. After returning from Babylon, the Israelites were determined to avoid the mistakes of their past and to remain faithful to the God of their ancestors.

To this end, the Israelites made a concerted effort to root out idolatry from their midst. This involved not only the destruction of idols and other symbols of false worship but also a renewed emphasis on the study of the Torah and the practice of the Jewish faith. The prophet Ezra played a key role in this effort, leading the people in a public reading of the Torah and calling on them to renew their commitment to God.

The impact of this renewed focus on God and the rejection of idolatry was profound. The Israelites were able to rebuild their temple and reestablish their religious practices, which served as a source of strength and unity for the Jewish people. They also developed a deeper appreciation for the importance of faith and the need to remain faithful to God, even in the face of adversity.

Another impact of Israel's experience with idolatry was that it reminded them of the dangers of turning away from God and reinforced their commitment to the Jewish faith. By rejecting false worship and rededicating themselves to the service of God, the Israelites were able to rebuild their community and establish a strong foundation for the future.

We in the modern world must learn and understand the principles of God and how He works. God is clear about what He desires. The body of Christ should also see, and it should be equally clear, how and why a nation goes into captivity. If we learn from history and apply the principles of God's Word, we will be set up to succeed and see a turnaround. God is calling His people out of a "Babylonian system" today just as He did in the days of ancient Israel!

THE SYSTEM OF BABYLON

We must bring God back into all areas of society again and reject the current system of Babylon. It blows my mind how many people buy into the false narrative of the modern-day prophets of Baal, also known as the mainstream corporate media (90 percent of which is owned by six corporations[3]), Hollywood, and the many voices who echo their erroneous and false reports. It's mainly propaganda and disinformation. They use these platforms to socially condition the masses—and many fall for it. We must come out of the Babylonian system and set ourselves apart by adhering to Scripture and standing fast to the principles of Christ's teachings. God has given us every single tool that we need in order to thrive. If we apply these tools and use the spiritual weapons God has given us, we will win every time!

These same people who have given themselves unto sin and wickedness are those who have sold out our country, similarly to how Judas sold out Jesus, for temporary wealth, status, prominence, acceptance, and creature comforts. Many of them have reprobate minds and no morality or belief in God at all. These are also the same people who would like to see the world population reduced by more than 70 percent, according to their own documents and speeches. This explains so much of what we see playing out today with the massive pushes for abortion, gay marriage and alternative lifestyles, gender confusion, and euthanasia. Notice how they all achieve the goal of fewer offspring and a reduced birth rate. This goes against God's desire for us to "be fruitful and multiply" (Gen. 1:28, ESV).

We are seeing the elites within the United Nations, the World Economic Forum, and other globalist organizations pushing a new world order and a globalist agenda, which is basically the same agenda behind the Tower of Babel in biblical times. As the Bible says, "There is nothing new under the sun" (Eccles. 1:9). Satan has been pushing this agenda through his demonic forces for centuries. His is a system of lies, distractions, anti-God ways, and corruption that moves in and exalts sin and immorality in a push for the beast system. It is a culture of death, which is the opposite of who God is, a God of life.

Satan distorts and counterfeits all that is of God. He operates in the principle that men can be like gods. In other words, we can take God out of the equation because we don't need Him. It's similar to the Oprah Winfrey–promoted book *The Secret*, which took aspects of a godly principle but left God out of the equation. It duped many people who thought they had been given some type of secret knowledge. It was a lie from the pit of hell!

Many elites and Luciferians (people given to the control of demons and demonic forces and ideas) are now trying to attain eternal life through science. This is why we are seeing a considerable push to connect humans with machines and to connect our brains electronically to the internet. This is a new frontier, and I don't think most Christians understand how this so-called fourth industrial revolution is set to challenge us like we have never been challenged before with regard to standing for our faith. The next decade will be a whole new level of this type of thing, and we had better prepare for it. People will be connecting themselves to the internet via tech and looking to enhance themselves in ways that just a few years ago would have been possible only in sci-fi movies.

The church must become proactive in order to face what is coming down the pike in the coming years—even before 2030. We need to learn to operate in big faith and truly trust the Lord. It will be unlike anything that we have seen in this generation. The time for us to develop this level of fortitude is now. I believe that if you have endured challenges in recent years and pressed through them, it's because God is strengthening His remnant and our ability to hold the line and pray things through to face what is yet to come.

ONE-WORLD GOVERNMENT PLAN IN PLACE

The push for a one-world global government has dramatically accelerated over the last few years. Many of the critical pieces are now being put into place, including the introduction of the CBDC (Central Bank Digital Currency) and global digital currency push. Those with discernment have an urgency in their spirits about this, as we know the hour is late and can see the enemy's plans are in full swing. I believe this is setting up the infrastructure for the beast system and the eventual rollout of the mark of the beast. Is your pastor talking about this? I hope so!

We are seeing a rise in the spirit of antichrist throughout the land. The Bible tells us even the elect will be deceived (Matt. 24:24). Believers must truly operate in wisdom and discernment as we prepare to navigate what is ahead. If we think the pressure to get the COVID-19 vaccine was intense, that will pale in comparison to the level of pressure the new-world-order globalists will apply to us in the years ahead as the digital currency system is introduced. We have already seen certain outspoken people deal with banks unexpectedly closing their accounts because they didn't meet the bank's standards.

This level of censorship and bias has only just begun. It started on social media but has now advanced to banking and other sectors, and the cancel culture will continue their push to try to stamp out conservative and Christian voices. This is why we are advocating for and working with many alternative organizations and companies to develop what we call "alternative ecosystems." This is a key way in which we will come out from among them.

These elites believe in what they call "making order out of chaos" and "problem-action-solution." They follow the books and teachings of men like Saul Alinsky, who wrote *Rules for Radicals*, a book that is literally dedicated to Lucifer! This is one of their playbooks, and we see its teachings in motion in today's Western world. Their solution is more government and further reliance and dependence on them instead of on God.

These elites want to push God out of everything. They make government and fabricated "science" their gods instead of the real God of heaven and earth! They always mix scientific theories in with facts; it's the only way they can bridge the gap between reality and their false version of reality. We see this in the push for evolution versus the actual truth of intelligent design. We also see this with the big bang theory versus the truth of what the Bible tells us: that God simply said, "Let there be light" (Gen. 1:3). They always have to fabricate in order to fill the missing link, yet they teach this theory as if it is fact.

This is how the devil tries to warp reality and discredit the Bible. This is the Babylonian system in full effect; it's modern-day Baal worship! Let's call a spade a spade.

Many churches refuse to speak on these issues, as they are deemed "controversial" or "conspiracy theories," which are terms that have been weaponized in order to keep people silent for fear of being ridiculed. Even when you can link directly to these elites' websites and speeches in which they lay out their plans for all the world to see, many will still refuse to acknowledge it.

Many people, Christians included, are walking in a mentality referred to as the "normalcy bias," meaning it is hard for them to believe these things are taking place or that anything will change. Despite the plethora of evidence available to anyone willing to research for themselves or to simply ask the Holy Spirit for wisdom and discernment, many remain inside the "matrix" of normalcy and don't think these things are actually happening.

Many people also trust these globalists to look out for their best interests. How many friends and relatives do you know who feel this way? As if these people care about our health and well-being because they use big words, show us power-point slides, and make elaborate presentations trying to convince us they are the good guys. Why in the world would anyone trust people who openly speak about the need for depopulation to want to save lives? To those with eyes to see, it's obvious something is very wrong. Others have unfortunately bought into the fear, lies, intimidation, and propaganda they are disseminating—even some Christians!

The globalists and deep-state players are pushing hard for chaos and confusion, for the destruction of family values and the family unit, *life*, biblical marriage, and common sense—total social breakdown. As I write this book, we see this in full motion throughout the United States and the West. Only a year or two ago many sat back and said almost nothing while our churches were called nonessential. At the same time, rebellious anarchists and paid agent provocateurs lit up many of our cities, rioted, burned down small businesses, and attacked police officers and their property. Lawlessness is of the enemy. He is called the lawless one!

Our nation is under attack in many ways. Our borders are open. Our children are under attack in their schools. Remarkably, we have allowed our country to get to this decrepit place. Where are the prominent Christian leaders? Why don't they sound the alarm about these things? Will there be an inflection point at which ordinary citizens will take up arms and push back? How close is our country to an actual civil war? More and more people are starting to ask these types of questions as the division has reached critical mass in recent years. It's not just about varying political views; there is a spiritual battle being waged before our eyes. This is a battle for the very soul of this nation. Even Joe Biden had this exact phrase, "Battle for the Soul of the

Nation," printed on his campaign bus ahead of the 2020 election. It's very much in our faces.

The many issues we are currently facing as a nation could be fixed, and there are natural solutions to each problem, yet most who are in positions of power instead continue to push ahead with the wicked plans in lockstep. These plans were never a good idea, have never worked before, and will not work now. They purposefully plunge us deeper into debt, darkness, and decline. At this point the only thing in their way is patriots like us and biblical Christianity! This is why they increasingly consider Christians to be a thorn in their side and Christian persecution in the West is rapidly increasing.

The globalists and elites promoting the Luciferian agenda can see that Bible-believing Christians who are spiritually astute and able to see the reality of the situation are the only ones with the spiritual authority to stop it, hence the increased friction. This became clear during the COVID pandemic when remnant leaders began to rise up and push back against their tyranny.

THE DEATH OF THE MEGACHURCH AND DENOMINATIONS?

What will the church look like in the years ahead? Will we continue to see what we are seeing now? Trends suggest that secularism is advancing and the church is declining. Is this true? There seem to be as many churches as coffee shops, one on the corner of almost every block in America, yet how much of an impact are we making? I say, not enough! Are the mainstream megachurches and woke churches who refuse to say or do anything about the issues we are facing deserving of our support any longer? Or should we be more careful about to whom we give? Are some churches receiving government funding and subsidies as long as they remain seeker-friendly and politically benign? I suggest supporting those who are in the battle and on the front lines instead. This is a war, folks! A spiritual war of light versus darkness. We need to establish a supply line that leads to the front line and those remnant pastors and leaders who are standing strong! This is something to prayerfully consider as we move ahead.

We cannot operate inside the elites' world of false reality any longer. This is why the church is meant to come out of this Babylonian system. A nation cannot stand without law, common sense, and most importantly, God. It's time to put God back into *everything*! This is the mandate of the rising remnant! *All Americans must understand where we are. America cannot survive without God!*

> And from the days of John the Baptist until now the kingdom of heaven suffereth violence, *and the violent take it by force.*
> —MATTHEW 11:12, KJV, EMPHASIS ADDED

We must take back this nation now by being active and involved in all areas of influence. If we think someone else will fix our problems, they won't. It's up to us, church! We must attend the community and school board meetings and get involved on both the local and national levels. We need to have a strong presence in all areas of society. The church needs to be an occupying force for righteousness. If not now, when? If not us, who? If not here, where? This is why you and I are alive at this hour! Everyone must do something.

Many of you have heard the call. Many have answered. It's time for the church to get back to making disciples. We also must be bold about fulfilling the Great Commission. We must be more dedicated than they are. Who are "they"? I mean the radical Left, globalists, and all those who are pushing this new world order and their anti-God agenda. We must win this spiritual battle for the soul of America! It's time for the silent majority to get off the bench and into the game.

Each of us has a part to play. We must never be silent or apathetic again. An estimated 64 percent of Americans identify as Christians.[4] We know that not all of these people are serving God, but think about how many people that is. In a nation of over 334 million people, roughly 213 million say they are Christians. So why have we given a small group of people so much power to continue to steer us into moral depravity? This is why we can't be in the middle. Each of us must choose a side. We Christians need to be vocal and let our voices be heard.

AN ANGELIC VISITATION AND A CALL TO CONSECRATION

You may be wondering, why am I so passionate about all this? In 2021, I experienced an angelic visitation. A messenger angel came and visited me in the middle of the night while I was asleep. It was quite the experience, and it rocked me to the core! I will never forget that night.

The angel said two things:

1. Come out from among them, and

2. Be consecrated.

Then the angel left. Over the next year I dug into that message and sought God as to what this means for the great body of Christ and for me personally.

I believe this is an hour of great shaking and awakening. Revival is at hand. It's the only hope for America and the West, as God is the only true hope for this world.

Faith without works is dead.

—JAMES 2:26, KJV

What does this look like, and how can we achieve this goal? What will the church look like in years to come? Will the modern-day megachurch morph into smaller tent gatherings, remnant churches, and home churches as the people of God wake up and realize that the seeker-friendly model may not be the answer when Christianity is under attack and our religious liberties and freedom hang in the balance? This is a time for remnant warriors to rise up and for the church to be who we are called to be. We cannot conform to the evil agenda and wickedness of this hour!

God is raising up a generation of lions and generals who are not afraid to take a stand for righteousness and push back against the woke mob mentality. What does this new generation of Christian leaders look like, and how can we take back the territory and culture for the kingdom of God? We will be discussing this in much more depth in the chapters ahead. This is a time for *big faith* and *big action*! We will not go out quietly. We will occupy until He comes!

ALTERNATIVE ECOSYSTEMS

The Christian world must start building alternative ecosystems and developing its own infrastructure. Home schools, health and wellness companies, insurance companies, banks, social media platforms—everything! We can no longer live and operate in a system that censors us, attacks our values, and forces a sinful lifestyle down our throats. Christians must come out from among them and be set apart in all we do.

While we are still in the world and certainly should keep ministering to nonbelievers, we cannot be controlled by those who wish to silence and suppress us. We must begin to act as if we are the majority—because we are! We also must be bold and vocal. We can't bow down to the pressure of cancel culture, which seeks to take away our ability to worship freely.

WHAT DOES IT MEAN TO STAND IN THE GAP?

To "stand in the gap" in prayer is a metaphorical expression that refers to interceding on behalf of others. The term comes from the Bible, specifically in the Book of Ezekiel where God is looking for someone to stand in the gap to prevent the destruction of Jerusalem. (See Ezekiel 22:30.) In this context, to stand in the gap means to intercede on behalf of the people, to plead for mercy, and to seek forgiveness.

Similarly, standing in the gap in prayer means to intercede on behalf of others who are in need, whether it be physical, emotional, or spiritual. It involves standing in the place of those who are in need and praying for God's intervention and mercy on their behalf. It can also involve confessing the sins of others and seeking God's forgiveness and healing for them. Standing in the gap in prayer is a selfless act of intercession where one puts the needs of another before his or her own and seeks God's intervention for the person's well-being.

While the Bible does not specifically mention praying for our country, it does encourage us to pray for our leaders and the welfare of our communities. In 1 Timothy 2:1–2 the apostle Paul writes, "I urge, then, first of all, that petitions, prayers, intercession and thanksgiving be made for all people—for kings and all those in authority, that we may live peaceful and quiet lives in all godliness and holiness."

This passage encourages believers to pray for those in leadership positions, including those who govern our nations, and to ask God for their guidance and wisdom. Additionally, in Jeremiah 29:7 the prophet instructs the Israelites to seek the welfare of the city to which they have been exiled and to pray to the Lord on its behalf. We must stand in the gap for our nation and the world.

There is much more we need to understand about how we come out from among them. My prayer is that you will be inspired by the Holy Spirit and set up for success as you continue to move forward and answer God's call on your life.

Christians must stand in the gap for America. We must learn to be prayer warriors and intercessors. This is one major way that we can come out from among them!

CHAPTER 3

THE PLAN OF THE ELITES

WHAT IS THE globalist agenda? Why should we care? One reason Christians are called to come out of this Babylonian system is because we are the ones who have the authority to stop it. Our prayers are a powerful weapon, and the Bible clearly tells us that we have the authority to pull down strongholds in the name of Jesus. We can also use the other tools God has given us such as fasting, declaring and decreeing, and speaking the truth of God's Word, which is the sword of the Spirit.

What are the plans of the elites and those who wish to silence voices of truth? Here are a few.

1. Encourage population control. Fund and push abortions worldwide. Fund and push euthanasia worldwide. Push the LGBTQ lifestyle through media, Hollywood, government, schools, textbooks, porn, and in all marketing channels. Saturate the system with images, and mainstream this lifestyle.

2. Create a borderless society. Erase national cultures, borders, and sovereignty. Push migration into Western countries and mix everything and everyone to eliminate any type of national identity/culture. One big melting pot (needed for the next stage). Undo Tower of Babel scattering. (The devil has always wanted a one-world government system so that the beast system can be implemented.)

3. Build a world system. Use the world court, world bank, UN, World Economic Forum, Interpol, world government, and world currency infrastructure (stage set). Push to go cashless in the near future to control buying and selling by means of the CDBC digital currencies which are already being rolled out in many countries. (Track it all.)

4. Put in place a monitoring system via technology. Use Facebook, social media, online tracking, and smartphones to make a file on every person on the planet using supercomputers and quantum computers. Track purchases, friends, and patterns. Utilize facial recognition. Track travel. Establish social credit score systems that push certain behaviors and punish others.

5. Push science and minimize Christian beliefs. Mainstream evolution. Mainstream science over intelligent design. Teach evolution as though it were a matter of fact. Use TV shows, movies, and documentaries to push this agenda. Deem biblical Christianity as antiquated, backward, a conspiracy, etc. Use weaponized words to describe truth-tellers and free thinkers.

6. Silence dissidents. Censor social media ministers and conservatives. Delist, deplatform, and ostracize. Use the media to attack these people.

7. Create corporate governance structures that operate outside of sovereign countries and constitutions. Push a new world order that usurps the authority of the Constitution and our freedoms and rights.

8. Send manufacturing and deep earth mineral resources to China. Establish China's military as a new global superpower and set the stage for China to have the power ("One Belt, One Road" initiative). Destabilize the US dollar and weaken the United States by outsourcing jobs, manufacturing base, and ability to produce military hardware in-house. Send classified military technology to China. Prepare the world for a new currency system when the dollar is unseated as a global reserve currency.

9. Classify biblical morality as hate speech, and silence and censor those who teach it. Biblical remnant pastors are now the target. Limit their ability to share by making key elements of core Christian doctrine and beliefs illegal under federal, state, and local laws. Use leftist organizations to label biblical preachers as hate-mongers and extremists.

10. Give the ports, Hollywood studios, and Panama Canal over to China in preparation for the next steps.

11. Control the money supply and ability to work so that anyone who opposes the new system can be cut off and financially sanctioned or isolated.

12. Make Christianity itself (its key foundations and

principles) illegal and label those who follow it enemies of the state (extremists, far-Right, conspiracy theorists, etc.).

13. Target the young people at an early age and have the schools teach them an alternative view of America as a racist, imperialist country that has harmed the world (a false narrative). Change history. Teach them to want socialism and hate capitalism. Foster an environment that pushes rebellion and anarchy. Teach them that law enforcement is bad and organizations like Antifa are good.

14. Disarm the population. Take away the citizens' guns so they cannot defend themselves against a tyrannical regime. (Think Venezuela or the rise of Nazi Germany.) They will have to first take away the guns in order to have full control, which is why this is a major part of their agenda and strategy.

15. Usurp and nullify the Constitution. The globalists want to take down the US Constitution and put us under a completely new system that would take away many of our current freedoms and rights.

You may think some of this is far off, but it's already underway! That's why the warfare is so intense. This is why we as Christians should be fervently fighting and pushing back against this plan right *now*! We also have to address it from the pulpit. We need to care about this, as it will greatly affect and change our lives.

Many people dismissed the same things during the 1930s before Hitler rose to power. History tends to repeat itself. We cannot simply operate in the normalcy bias thinking these things can't happen here, as they most certainly can, and the plan is well underway. Look into the writings of Dietrich Bonhoeffer, whom I will discuss later in this book, and you may be startled to see the similarities between much of what is happening in America right now and issues he sounded the alarm about in Germany during those days. My prayer is that we respond differently than the many people who chose to ignore his warnings.

THE TRANSGENDER MOVEMENT

This whole transgender movement that has been pushed by the leftists and socialists serves a purpose. It is important that we realize why this is happening and what their greater objective is.

1. It usurps, stands against, and distorts the biblical family unit. The enemy is known for perverting the truth and the original pure intention and order of things established by God. The Bible tells us to be fruitful and multiply (Gen. 1:28). This concept is robbed from humanity when it is allowed to be distorted in the false teachings of "acceptance" and "gender reassignment." Gender cannot be changed. A person is born either a man or a woman, and this is a proven fact. Trust the science, right? There are two chromosomes, X and Y. That's it!

2. It serves as a catalyst to implement the constructs of agenda 2030 and global population

reduction. If fewer people procreate, the population will begin to plummet, which is a goal of the global elite. We are already seeing this happen in several countries. In tandem with the massive push for alternative lifestyles that do not allow for human reproduction, a massive amount of estrogen mimickers that chemically alter our normal hormonal balance has been introduced into our food supply.[1] This is one of the reasons that men's sperm counts continue to fall—this generation of men has the lowest in history (since records have been taken).[2] This adds to the goal of more-feminized men and fewer offspring. This is not just an idea but a real issue that has been proven and is currently in motion.

3. The global elites and social leftists/communists are using the Muslim religion to help achieve their goals. Rich Higgins, director for strategic planning for the US national security adviser, was recently fired for the memo he wrote exposing this very plan.[3] Many Muslims have been strategically placed throughout the Western world thanks to initiatives designed to resettle refugees from war-torn nations such as Somalia. These policies were backed by the Obama administration and global elites who used nongovernmental organizations (NGOs) to implement them. Using Saul Alinsky's methods in unison with the deep state, the globalists destabilized Muslim countries in the Middle East during the Arab Spring in an effort to cause a mass migration into Western societies. This is why we have seen a major influx of migrants in Europe and even parts of the US.

The blending of Western culture is well underway and is part of a much greater agenda of globalization. Muslims have one of the highest birth rates of any religious group, and researchers believe there will be more babies born to Muslim mothers than to Christians by the year 2035.[4] This will have a deep impact on the social order of Western and global culture in the coming years and decades. From a spiritual standpoint this will have a major impact not only on Christians but also on Jews. The central planners know what they are doing.

This is all being done to continue to push society, the world, and our children and future generations away from Judeo-Christian values and morals and into a new global order. The elites want to rob us of our rightful place and identity as believers, and they will continue to use this strategy to implement a one-world global government and state religion.

This is similar to what we have seen in Communist China, as I believe China is a testing ground for many of the policies they would like to eventually roll out globally. China has put tremendous restrictions on its citizens and has been draconian in its efforts to control its population during the COVID era. China has a state-sanctioned church, which greatly limits the ability to teach and preach the full Bible. This is what the elites will soon be pushing in the Western world as well.

At some point the real church, the remnant, will most likely be forced to go underground much like the true church in China. Most Americans don't realize just how close this is to becoming reality in the Western world. Many of you have a sense of urgency in your heart. That has been put there by God. Don't doubt the still, small voice that is speaking to you. This is why we must use wisdom and discernment from the Holy Spirit to navigate in the years to come.

This is all biblical. The Bible is literally coming to life before our eyes as many prophecies are starting to manifest right in front of us. Whether or not we have the eyes to see and ears to hear is up to us! No, it isn't "hate"—this information is true and the product of a sober mind. And the truth is what sets the captive free.

THE SOCIAL CREDIT SCORE SYSTEM AND THE MARK OF THE BEAST

The concept of a social credit score system has been gaining traction in recent years. It is already being implemented in China.[5] The idea behind this system is to assign a score to each individual based on his or her behavior, actions, and other factors with the aim of encouraging positive behavior and discouraging negative behavior.

There are concerns, however, that the social credit score system could eventually turn into the mark of the beast as described in the Book of Revelation. The mark of the beast is a symbol associated with the Antichrist, and it is said that those who receive the mark will be damned for all eternity.

The similarities between the social credit score system and the mark of the beast are striking. Both involve assigning a number to each individual, and both are intended to exert control over people's behavior. The social credit score system is designed to encourage people to act in certain ways, while the mark of the beast is described as a tool for controlling people's minds and souls.

One of the key concerns about the social credit score system is that it could be used to enforce conformity and suppress dissent by restricting people's freedoms and controlling their behavior. In China, for example, individuals who express dissenting views and have a low social credit score may be prevented from traveling, accessing certain services, or even finding employment. This kind of control over people's lives and speech is reminiscent of the control that the Antichrist is said to exert over his followers.

It is important to note that the social credit score system is not inherently evil or malevolent. It is intended to encourage positive behavior and discourage negative behavior, and in many cases, it may be effective in achieving these goals. However, there is a risk that the system could be abused or used for nefarious purposes, and it is important to remain vigilant and ensure that it is used in a responsible and ethical manner.

THE BEAST SYSTEM

The term *beast system* is not explicitly used in the Bible. However, it is a concept that is often associated with the Book of Revelation in the New Testament. Revelation 13 describes a beast rising out of the sea that is said to have authority over the earth.

This beast is often interpreted as a symbol of a future political power or kingdom that will rise up and exert control over the world. This kingdom is sometimes called the beast system or the antichrist system. The Book of Revelation also speaks of a false prophet who will lead people to worship the beast, and those who do not worship the beast will face persecution.

Interpretations of the meaning of the beast system vary widely among different Christian denominations and theologians. Some believe the beast system is a literal future entity, while others interpret it as a metaphor for the evil and corruption that has existed throughout human history. Based on my study and research, I believe it is a literal entity.

Revelation 13:1–2 describes a beast with ten horns and seven heads rising out of the sea. This beast is often interpreted as a symbol of a political system or empire, and the ten horns may represent ten kings or kingdoms.

Similarly, Revelation 17:3–14 describes a woman riding a beast with ten horns. The horns represent ten kings who will receive power along with the beast for a brief time. This woman is often identified as a symbol of a false religious system or city and the beast as a symbol of a political system.

Interpretations of the identity of the ten kings or kingdoms vary among different schools of thought. Some interpret them as a future political alliance of ten nations, while others view them as a historical or symbolic representation of various empires or kingdoms.

The Antichrist and the mark of the beast are found in the New Testament of the Bible, particularly in the Book of Revelation.

The Antichrist is a figure who is often described as a great deceiver and adversary of Christ. The word *antichrist* is not used frequently in the Bible, but it is generally understood to refer to a person or a group of people who oppose Christ and His teachings. Some scholars believe that the Antichrist is a specific individual who will appear at the end of time, while others interpret the Antichrist as a more symbolic representation of evil.

The mark of the beast, also mentioned in Revelation, is a mark that is said to be placed on the forehead or right hand of those who worship the Antichrist. It is described as a way for the Antichrist to control and identify his followers. Those who refuse to receive the mark are said to be persecuted and may be put to death.

Interpretations of the mark of the beast vary widely. Some view it as a literal mark that will be placed on people in the end times, while others see it as a symbol of allegiance to the Antichrist or as a metaphor for the way that people can be controlled by worldly power. This is the first time in history that the technology is available for people to actually receive a mark or chip that could allow them to purchase goods or have their ability to transact taken away by those in power. This is why there is an urgency in the hearts of those who discern the lateness of the hour and are able to connect biblical prophecy to many things currently taking place or being set up.

The idea that the elites and those who hate God would want to form a one-world global government, much like they are doing right now, is not so far-fetched. While many will call you a conspiracy theorist for thinking or believing this, those who walk in discernment and understand the lateness of the hour realize that this plan is already well underway and in its late stages. As people of God, we must not let those who mock us or call us crazy get under our skin. The Bible has an impeccable track record, and what we are explaining in this chapter is factual and real. This is another important reason we must come out from among them and listen clearly to the voice of the Lord.

CHAPTER 4

THE GREAT REPRIEVE

WHEN PRESIDENT DONALD J. Trump was elected the 45th president of the United States in 2016, many spoke of a season of "great reprieve." Whether you liked President Trump or not, God allowed a season during which religious liberties and freedoms were protected under his watch, as he was very friendly to the church and overall Christian community. His policy stances made this clear. He also surrounded himself with many of the nation's prominent Christian leaders, who formed what was known as his faith advisory board.

Many believe that due to the prayers of the righteous, God gave the church in America some more time to get people saved, set free, healed, and delivered. He gave us more time to awaken those who have been deceived. The question is, How did we steward that time? Is the body of Christ doing what we must to make a difference? We have the authority in the name of Jesus to pull down strongholds. We can cancel the assignment of hell against the nation and the world. Has the church in America and the West stepped up and changed the broken patterns and ways that we had prior to the Trump era?

As I have written for many years on this topic, it was never about Donald J. Trump. Although many people like to critique, criticize, and analyze his every move, I don't believe that is what God is concerned about. We shouldn't be either. In my view, God gave His church a chance to *correct its course* during the Trump era and focus on souls.

During this time, God started to really separate the wheat from the tares. The harvest has always been the center of God's heart. The Western church has become too focused on church growth strategies and the overall megachurch environment. This has resulted in a "wide gate," hyper-grace, seeker-friendly Christian culture that I believe has done tremendous damage and is a good reason why we're in the position we are in today.

What happened in 2016 was a direct response to the prayers of the righteous remnant in America and worldwide who had been crying out to God for revival and another Great Awakening. I believe it was a last-minute reprieve, a period during which God was willing to show His mercy, grace, and love and give us a little more time to get it right—one more round, if you will. (I'll explain this later in this chapter.) We are still in that period, but the hour is growing late and time is running out. How long will this season of grace remain? We see the warning signs all around us. We know the wicked are busy making plans and strategizing about how they can rein in those who are willing to stand for righteousness. The culture war, which is really a spiritual war, is reaching its apex.

This period of reprieve was given to the American people, but mostly to the American church. The spotlight is on us now. *"If My people..."* God wants His body to respond in accordance with His will. We can't return to business as usual. We need all hands on deck.

We have seen decades of moral decline, a prolonged anti-God/anti-Christianity movement, and a culture of death that celebrates the murder of our most innocent members of society—our babies. Let's face it, our culture has been walking in utter rebellion for quite some time. We must wake up. This is one of the main reasons God put it on my heart to write this book. I am not holding back, as I feel an extreme sense of urgency for the body of Christ to understand what is at stake.

Our mandate is simple:

1. Do not act like it's business as usual! We must repent for the apathy and complacency that we have walked in for years and turn from these ways. We have to stop making church a show, get back to the heart of worship, and boldly teach the truth.

2. Stand for the Bible. We can't cherry-pick or leave out portions of the Bible, water down Scripture, or be afraid of losing church members. We are simply the messengers. We are meant to be salt and light in the world. It is truth that sets the captive free! We must make disciples and raise up a generation of young lions who have the fortitude to push back against the demonic "woke" agenda and cancel culture that have invaded our nation and the church like a cancerous plague.

3. Make it about souls. We must occupy until the Lord comes. We must return to biblical evangelism. If we do this right, the nation will be saved. If we miss the mark here, there is little chance we will win.

GOD IS GIVING HIS PEOPLE DREAMS AND VISIONS

Many people are getting downloads from God prophetically. Some are speaking of possible calamity and of great tribulations that we could soon see in America. Their message is we either repent now, or we could see a time unlike we have ever seen in our history. Others are speaking of a coming revival, a great awakening and a powerful move of God. We are already beginning to see signs of this revival.

I believe these prophetic downloads will increase as we press in deeper. It is my prayer that God will give us more time. God has shown me it is time that we get comfortable about being uncomfortable. We have to step out of the boat, look Jesus in the eye, and walk on water. The answer is not in a political movement or politician, but rather that the body of Christ must rise up and take a true stand for righteousness.

Think of the many pivotal times in history when people had to take a stand for what is right. I think of men like Abraham Lincoln and Thomas Jefferson. Dr.

Martin Luther King Jr. and so many others also took a great risk and put everything on the line to defend what is right and true. Our generation has had it pretty easy in comparison, as for the most part we haven't had to take these stands until now. We need to understand that the times have shifted and the environment today is much different from what it was even twenty years ago.

My grandfather was a veteran of World War II and has now gone to be with the Lord. I often wonder how he would look at the cultural and spiritual situation we now face. He would have thought many of these "new social norms" were absolutely insane and wicked— because they are! Yet for some reason many Christians have been duped into accepting these wicked agendas instead of pushing back and taking the needed stand against them.

God will respond to the prayers of the righteous, but first we must repent and be sincere in fulfilling our mission as the body of Christ. There is an attack of division and fear striking our nation right now. God tells us very specifically in His Word that He "has not given us a spirit of fear, but of power and of love and of a sound mind" (2 Tim. 1:7, NKJV). We must walk in wisdom and use discernment to navigate all that is currently going on. We must be bold and willing to hold fast to what the Bible says, no matter how hard the pressure is against us. We must be empowered by the Holy Spirit to get clear direction from God. This is why each of us must have an active prayer life and also spend time in the secret place (Ps. 91).

"ONE MORE ROUND"

With the expanding war in Eastern Europe, the recent global pandemic, societal breakdowns worldwide, and so many significant geopolitical challenges around the globe, one could start to seriously question if we are on the verge of total calamity as a civilization. Will America—and freedom worldwide—endure and rise once again? Are the days of the American "Eagle" numbered?

This is a question I have been seriously asking the Lord in recent months, as we certainly need divine wisdom, strategy, and intervention in this late hour. We also need revelation and discernment that only God can give us. What happens in America affects the entire globe. The world is watching.

China could realistically move in and change the entire global financial order in the very near future. We know the World Economic Forum has been talking about a diminished United States and a nefarious plan they call the Great Reset. There are so many variables right now as to how this plan could be implemented and rolled out. Some are already well underway.

We see a shifting global order and the possibility of a new financial system rising in the years ahead. The US dollar has been the global reserve currency since Bretton Woods, but we are now seeing a major crack in the ceiling of the dollar's hegemony. What will happen if and when the US loses its global reserve status? How will our lives be affected?

Looking in the natural, there is no shortage of things to be concerned about. One could certainly be over-whelmed reading the latest headlines or listening to the corporate media's propagandized narrative. My advice: tune them out!

But God...

After much fasting and prayer, I hear God saying, *"The time is not yet! We shall have one more round!"*

It's time to speak to the dry bones! We declare and decree that America shall *live*! We cannot lose hope or give up. We lose the battle only when we give up and surrender. This is why the enemy is pushing so hard against so many of us. He wants us to grow weary and feel isolated, defeated, and alone. We cannot buy into these lies! The apostle Paul talked about encouraging ourselves in Christ. I believe this is something each and every Christian must learn to do in this hour. This is why having a daily prayer life is so important.

It is crucial that we take all of this seriously in this hour, as the time is growing short. We can no longer afford to mess around; that time has passed. This is a moment for sobriety, a moment in which we must really hunger for God. We also need to close any open doors of sin in our lives and families because if we don't, the enemy will use them. We must consecrate ourselves in this time and truly set ourselves apart from the evil the world is pushing.

I have to trust the voice of the Lord. Despite what the headlines read, God is telling me and many others that we are not yet done as a nation or a people. But there are strings attached; we must do our part. Through this book I am not only speaking the truth about the evil that is going on but also laying out the strategy by which we can overcome this evil and be the body of Christ that the Lord desires us to be according to His Word.

THE SEVEN CHURCHES

The Book of Revelation, the final book of the New Testament, includes messages from Jesus Christ to seven churches. (See Revelation chapters 2 and 3.) It is critical that we understand what the Spirit said to each of these churches, as we see the same issues addressed in the seven churches playing out before our eyes in America today.

These churches were located in seven cities in the ancient Roman province of Asia (present-day Turkey) and were believed to be the primary centers of Christianity in the region during the time when the Book of Revelation was written. The seven churches are as follows:

1. Ephesus (Rev. 2:1–7): The first church mentioned was located in the city of Ephesus, which was a major port city and center of trade. The church in Ephesus was commended for its hard work and perseverance, but it was also criticized for having left its first love and for allowing false teachings to enter the church.

2. Smyrna (Rev. 2:8–11): The second church mentioned was located in the city of Smyrna, which was a wealthy and influential city. The church in Smyrna was commended for its faithfulness in the face of persecution and poverty, and it was warned that it would suffer more persecution and trials.

3. Pergamum (Rev. 2:12–17): The third church mentioned was located in the city of Pergamum, which was a center of pagan worship and the imperial cult. The church in Pergamum was commended for its faithfulness in the face of persecution, but it was also criticized for allowing false teachings and immorality to enter the church.

4. Thyatira (Rev. 2:18–29): The fourth church mentioned was located in the city of Thyatira, which was a center of trade and commerce. The church in Thyatira was commended for its love, faith, service, and perseverance, but it was also criticized for allowing false teachings and immorality to enter the church.

5. Sardis (Rev. 3:1–6): The fifth church mentioned was located in the city of Sardis, which was a wealthy and prosperous city. The church in Sardis was criticized for being spiritually dead and urged to wake up and strengthen what remained.

6. Philadelphia (Rev. 3:7–13): The sixth church mentioned was located in the city of Philadelphia, which was a center of agriculture and trade. The church in Philadelphia was commended for its faithfulness and perseverance and was promised that it would be kept from the hour of trial that would come upon the whole world.

7. Laodicea (Rev. 3:14–22): The seventh and final church mentioned was located in the city of Laodicea, which was a wealthy and prosperous city known for its banking industry. The church in Laodicea was criticized for being lukewarm and urged to repent, and it was promised that those who overcome would sit with Christ on His throne.

Each of the seven churches had its unique strengths and weaknesses, and each received a message from Jesus Christ through the apostle John urging its people to repent, overcome their weaknesses, and hold fast to their faith. These messages were not only relevant to the churches of the time, but they also serve as timeless lessons and warnings for all Christians throughout history.

Isn't it interesting that right now we are literally witnessing what John was shown in the Book of Revelation in the greater body of Christ? It's very important that we take these things into account, pray, and remember that God said He would spit out the lukewarm (Rev. 3:16). "Small is the gate and narrow the road" to salvation (Matt. 7:14). We must apply Scripture and understand why God shared these things with us to ensure that our walk with Christ is sustainable for the long term. Scripture tells us that we must finish well. It also specifically mentions those who "endure until the end" (Matt. 24:13). The Christian walk is a long game—not a sprint but a marathon. We must stay the course and stay on mission.

REVIVAL HISTORY

Throughout history we have seen a series of Holy Spirit-led movements known as Christian revivals. These movements are characterized by an increased interest in Christianity, an emphasis on personal conversion, and a renewal of spiritual fervor. Revivals have occurred in different parts of the world and at different times, but they all share a common goal: to bring people back to God and to help them experience a renewed sense of purpose and direction in their lives. Let's explore some of the most significant Christian revivals in history.

The First Great Awakening (1730s–1740s)

The first Great Awakening was a religious revival that took place in the American colonies in the 1730s and 1740s. It was led by influential preachers such as George Whitefield and Jonathan Edwards, who emphasized the importance of personal conversion and a direct relationship with God. The revival had a significant impact on American society, as it led to the establishment of new churches and the rise of Evangelicalism as a major force in American religious life.

The Second Great Awakening (early nineteenth century)

The second Great Awakening was a revival that took place in the United States in the early nineteenth century. It was marked by the rise of new religious groups such as the Mormons and the Seventh-day Adventists, as well as the growth of Evangelicalism and the establishment of many new churches. The revival also had a significant impact on social and political issues such as the abolitionist movement and the push for women's suffrage.

The Welsh Revival (1904–1905)

The Welsh Revival was a religious revival that took place in Wales in 1904 and 1905. It was led by the preacher Evan Roberts, who emphasized the importance of personal conversion and deepening one's relationship with God. The revival had a significant impact on Welsh society and led to a surge in church attendance and the establishment of new churches. It also had a profound impact on Welsh culture, as it inspired a new wave of Welsh-language literature and music.

The Azusa Street Revival (1906–1915)

The Azusa Street Revival was a revival that began in Los Angeles, California, in 1906. It was led by the preacher William J. Seymour, who emphasized the importance of the Holy Spirit and the gift of tongues. The revival had a significant impact on American Christianity, as it helped to popularize Pentecostalism as a distinct branch of Christianity. It also had a profound impact on global Christianity, inspiring the growth of Pentecostal and Charismatic movements around the world.

The East African Revival (1930s–1950s)

The East African Revival was a religious revival that took place in East Africa in the 1930s–1950s. It was led by a group of African Christian leaders who emphasized the importance of personal conversion, holiness, and deepening one's relationship with God. The revival had a significant impact on African Christianity, as it led to the establishment of new churches and the growth of Evangelicalism as a major force in African religious life.

The Jesus Movement (1960s–1970s)

The Jesus movement revival took place in the United States in the 1960s–1970s. It was led by a group of young people who emphasized the importance of personal conversion and a new approach to Christian spirituality. The revival had a significant impact on American Christianity, as it led to the establishment of new churches and the growth of nondenominational Christianity as a major force in American religious life.

The Toronto Blessing (1990s)

The Toronto Blessing was a revival movement that began in January 1994 at the Toronto Airport Vineyard

Church (renamed the Toronto Airport Christian Fellowship, or TACF, in 1996)[1] in Toronto, Canada. It was a Charismatic movement that brought about significant changes in the way people worshipped and expressed their faith.

The Toronto Blessing was characterized by an outpouring of the Holy Spirit that was marked by manifestations such as uncontrollable laughter, shaking, crying, and falling to the ground. These manifestations were often accompanied by healing, prophecies, and other spiritual experiences.

The TACF became the center of the Toronto Blessing movement, drawing in people from all over the world who wanted to experience the revival. The movement gained worldwide attention and sparked controversy among Christians, with some questioning the authenticity of the experiences and others embracing it as a move of God.

The Toronto Blessing also had a significant impact on worship practices, with the emphasis shifting toward a more experiential and spontaneous form of worship. This led to the emergence of a new genre of worship music, known as "praise and worship," which incorporated the experiences and expressions of the Toronto Blessing movement.

Despite the controversies and criticisms, the Toronto Blessing movement continued to spread and influence the wider Christian community. It inspired many other

Charismatic movements, and its impact can still be seen today in the form of contemporary Christian worship and the ongoing pursuit of spiritual experiences.

The Brownsville Revival (1995–2000)

The Brownsville Revival, also known as the Pensacola Outpouring, was a Christian revival that began at the Brownsville Assembly of God church in Pensacola, Florida, in 1995. The revival lasted for several years and attracted thousands of people from all over the world who were seeking spiritual renewal and a deeper connection with God.

The revival was led by evangelist Steve Hill, who had previously worked as a missionary in Argentina and had experienced a powerful spiritual awakening there. Hill was invited to speak at the Brownsville Assembly of God church in 1995, and his message ignited a fire among the congregation. People began to have intense spiritual experiences, including speaking in tongues, healings, and visions.

The revival quickly spread beyond the walls of the Brownsville Assembly of God church and became a global phenomenon. People came from all over the world to attend the nightly services and experience the power of the Holy Spirit. The services were characterized by intense worship, passionate preaching, and powerful manifestations of the Holy Spirit.

One of the most notable features of the Brownsville Revival was the altar call that was given at the end of each service. Thousands of people would come forward to the altar to receive prayer and seek spiritual renewal. Many people reported experiencing physical and emotional healing, and many others were filled with the Holy Spirit and spoke in tongues.

The Brownsville Revival also had a significant impact on the local community. The church became a hub for social services, offering food, clothing, and shelter to those in need. The revival also led to the formation of several new ministries, including a drug and alcohol rehabilitation program and a prison ministry.

Despite its many successes, the Brownsville Revival was not without controversy. Some critics accused the revival of being overly emotional and lacking in theological depth. Others questioned the authenticity of the healings and spiritual experiences that were reported.

The revival eventually came to an end in the year 2000, although many of the ministries that were born out of the revival continue to this day. The impact of the Brownsville Revival on the global Christian community is still felt today, with many churches and ministries modeling their services and outreach programs after the Brownsville model.

The Brownsville Revival was a powerful Christian movement that had a significant impact on the global Christian community. Despite the controversy, it is clear that it touched the lives of thousands of people who were seeking spiritual renewal and a deeper connection with

God. The legacy of the Brownsville Revival continues to inspire and challenge Christians around the world to seek after God with all their heart, soul, and mind.

REVIVAL TODAY

Revival starts with each of us examining our own hearts and getting to a place of true surrender before the Lord. Imagine if the body of Christ did this as a whole. For years many have sought to operate in a form of godliness while still holding on to key aspects of their former life of sin. In many churches this acceptance has been the norm rather than confronting areas of sin in love. Many pastors have lost their desire and the tenacity to stand firm on God's Word and hold the sheep accountable. Let's face it: many pastors are living in sin themselves.

On the corporate side of things, I have seen churches spend millions of dollars (church resources) to put on large events, many of which weren't even focused on or related to the harvest. I'm not saying this is always the case, but I've seen it enough times to mention it. I believe this grieves the Lord. It is time for the body of Christ to make some adjustments and get back to the main mission of the church. We also need to reintroduce accountability, mentorship, and discipleship.

God wants all of us to go into the deep end of our walk with Christ. Deeper waters are where we finally lay down those areas of compromise we have carried with us throughout our walk and get serious. As we go deeper in our faith, we will see the wells of revival beginning to open up more and more.

Scripture tells us, "Deep calls unto deep" (Ps. 42:7, NKJV). God is calling His *ecclesia* (church) to move into a new-wineskin season of depth and maturity. We need to desire the "meat" in our faith walk, not just stay at level one. It's critical that we go deeper into God's Word during this time, as it is a lamp unto our feet. The Bible tells us that faith comes from hearing the Word of God. (See Romans 10:17.) So many churches barely even dig into Scripture, and instead their pastors preach very basic, motivational types of messages. This is part of a greater problem that I call "microwave Christianity." I know people who have been in churches for years and have never spoken to their pastor even one time. That is unacceptable. We need true shepherds who have a love for people leading their flocks.

For America, repentance is a must. God shared with me that when repentance becomes mainstream, at least within the true church, and we hear this word being preached all around the country, we will see full-blown revival! Why did we stop preaching such things, anyway? It's so important that we teach and preach about the blood of Jesus, repentance of sin, the cross of Calvary, purity, and holiness! The microwave Christianity messages of hyper-grace and motivational bliss will start to fade as people seek real lions and generals in the pulpit.

We began seeing this during the COVID era as people

sought leaders who were willing to take a stand and not bow down to government overreach and tyranny. Both small and larger remnant-type congregations witnessed exponential growth during and after COVID, while many of those who shut down for long periods of time or who didn't take a stand witnessed their congregation sizes substantially diminish. People could no longer look to many of the leaders of old who so quickly caved and bowed to unconstitutional mandates and a clear demonic plan to attempt to shut down the church.

It blew my mind that strip clubs and Walmart were open while churches were deemed "nonessential." And doesn't that just speak volumes about the state the church was in at that time, that our government could deem us nonessential and pastors and many Christians would be OK with that description? It's time for the real church, the essential church, to rise up! The Laodicean churches may in fact be nonessential, but the Philadelphian church certainly is needed—especially right now!

The Bible says the forces of evil will be overcome by "the blood of the Lamb and by the word of [our] testimony" (Rev. 12:11). We must turn from our wickedness and return to our first love, Jesus Christ. There is no path to restoring America other than a repentant people of God wholeheartedly turning back to the King of kings and Lord of lords! The American people are being given a chance similar to what God allowed in ancient Nineveh. However, if we do not heed the word of the Lord and correct our course as a nation and the body of Christ, we could go down the path of Sodom and Gomorrah or into captivity like ancient Israel. Our very freedom is at stake. Everything is on the line here.

This entire post–2020 election period has been a shaking. God is using this time to separate the wheat from the chaff and make it clear who is who. The church is being shaken out of its apathy and complacency. We could no longer do business as usual; something had to change! We could not go on the way we were. This is why God has allowed this period of time, even though it has been very uncomfortable and quite disruptive. God is using this time to get our attention. It's all about the church and the people of God. The Lord will come back for a church with neither spot nor wrinkle (Eph. 5:27).

Although things appear to be similar to how the Bible describes the end, the end is not yet. God, in His infinite grace and mercy, is allowing us this additional time. The enemy is counterfeiting what the end will be like in an attempt to paralyze the body of Christ and riddle us with fear. We must recognize this assignment of hell and rise above it into our true identity as a victorious people and children of the most high God. Complete victory! Think 2 Chronicles 20. God goes before us, but we must also take our position and stand.

It is critical that the body of Christ heed this important warning. The good news is there is still one more round. We are not done! We are not defeated! We can still turn this thing around! The end is *not* yet!

While all of this is playing out, I believe we will also see the greatest spiritual harvest in the history of the world. We are on the cusp of this harvest, and in many places it has already begun. Many are catching the fire and hearing the voice of God in dreams and visions. Many have urgency in their spirits and know through discernment that something significant is taking place. We are already in revival!

It is not the church's mission to attempt to be "relevant." Jesus is always relevant! We must walk in the full counsel of God. We must operate in boldness and authority!

God is calling the misfits.

He is calling the underdogs.

He is calling the prodigals.

He is calling those who feel rejected.

He is calling His bride to "come out from among them" and to consecrate herself.

God is ready to anoint Davids and appoint Esthers in this hour, those who appear the least likely to be raised up. Watch for this! It is the humble and contrite who will be accelerated—the pure streams! This isn't about one person or a particular name or ministry. This is all about Jesus!

We will see people who don't look like the stereotypical Christian coming forward to accept Jesus as their Lord and Savior. Many will have tattoos and piercings. Many will be coming off hard-core drug and alcohol addictions. These are the people whom God is calling in this hour along with everyone else. It will be hard for religious types to accept this, as it will appear "messy." Millions of unchurched people will soon be coming into a relationship with Jesus Christ. We have to be ready for this type of harvest. I've watched this happen for the last couple of years, but it is accelerating. The church will look different than it has for many years. This harvest will include the least likely people, many of whom will leave their drug sacks and pipes at the altar and have a radical encounter with the living God.

We will also see a convergence on key revival epicenters, certain hubs that will experience an open heaven and a great outpouring of the Holy Spirit in miracles, signs, and wonders. This will then flow out to all corners of the globe. Those who come against the church in this hour will be taken down. Don't touch the church! Also, the counterfeits will be exposed. God will not be mocked! Look for even more exposure to come.

This is the hour of the rising remnant. Those who are willing to adhere to the full counsel of God. Those who hunger and thirst for righteousness and are not afraid of holiness! Those who are anointed by God will thrive as they accept their calling and walk in the authority, anointing, and favor of God despite what is going on around them.

It is the anointing that breaks the yoke of bondage. God has called us to occupy until He comes! He will be with us, even until the end of the age. He will never leave us nor forsake us.

It's time for all fivefold ministry giftings to work in a godly order and unity in the ecclesia. For years, not all giftings have been celebrated and allowed to flow in their optimal calling due to a religious spirit in the church. God wants to move in a mighty way in this hour. We must get out of His way and not quench the Holy Spirit.

It is by the grace of God that we have been given more time. It is important that we understand the significance of the time we are in and make the most of this opportunity.

- Cast down fear.

- Cast down doubt.

- Call upon the name of the Lord!

- Repent of any open doors or areas of sin.

- Expect miracles.

- Have big faith.

- Be bold.

- Trust in the Lord.

If God is calling you, step up! Be like the prophet Isaiah and say, "Send me; I'll go." (See Isaiah 6:8.) Our job is to show up. The hour is late. We are meant to go out, cast out, and drive out! This is the church's greatest hour! We were made for a time such as this! This is our opportunity to go deeper with God than ever before, to really press in. This is the hour of the remnant. This is the time to stand!

CHAPTER 5

THE GREAT SHAKING

HISTORY TENDS TO repeat itself. As the Bible says in Ecclesiastes 1:9, there is nothing new under the sun. As I have already mentioned, the world is experiencing a shaking unlike anything this generation has seen. There is social unrest erupting all around the world. The mainstream media is not covering much of it because they don't want us to know that a global populace is awakening. People are waking up in droves and starting to see the wicked plans of the elites play out, plans that have been hidden for decades but are now being exposed for us to clearly see.

The internet has opened a whole new frontier for the gathering of information and the sharing of truth. While much truth is coming to the surface, a great deal of disinformation and misinformation is being shared as well. This is why it's more important than ever that we operate in discernment. Many Christians have fallen victim to the deceptions that are packaged well and appear to be Christian. This is why the Bible tells us we must "test the spirits" (1 John 4:1). Men are saying they are women, and women are claiming to be men. There is an attack on gender and biblical marriage. Babies are being ripped from their mothers' wombs in the form of late-term abortion while millions celebrate, claiming they have the right to do so.

Wicked leaders have been put into positions of power worldwide and at all levels of governance. We are currently witnessing this in the United States, where many believers are convinced that the elections themselves, as well as the voting systems, have been significantly corrupted and are able to manipulate even who is put into office. While it has been deemed a conspiracy, the possibility of something like this happening in some capacity is very real. This is why many remnant people feel such a heaviness and have been challenged in this season to pray harder than ever before. We all sense something is very wrong.

Good is being called evil and evil is being called good, just as the Bible told us would happen as the hour gets late (Isa. 5:20; 2 Tim. 3:13). Many people are wondering what will happen next. The church will endure until the Lord returns! Even if nations fall or the world order is significantly altered, there will be a body of Christ on the earth when the Lord returns for His bride. We must have the faith needed to endure until the end.

> Your kingdom is an everlasting kingdom, and your dominion endures throughout all generations.
> —Psalm 145:13, esv

Despite this assurance that the body of Christ will endure, many Christians are still concerned about their future and are battling anxiety or depression. Depression is a spirit that comes upon a person, and we must recognize it for what it is and cast it down in Jesus' name. It is important that we operate in the Lord's peace and learn to cast down our burdens at the foot of the cross.

As we witness some of our brothers and sisters lose their jobs and reputations due to their beliefs and cancel culture, we also continue to see Christianity being pushed out of schools and educational institutions. Our kids are a major target. The evil players in this world are making a significant effort to target children at a young age and indoctrinate them with demonic and unholy propaganda. This has become more important to many of the nation's school systems than actually educating these kids and setting them up for success.

The indoctrination of our young people has reached such a level of critical mass that we are now seeing a major uptick in homeschooling by concerned parents who don't want to see their kids indoctrinated by an out-of-control state. Witnessing this, and sometimes feeling overwhelmed by it, we are rightfully alarmed. We haven't experienced this before, and most Christians in the West have not been taught by their church leaders how to spiritually endure the things that are happening in our culture today.

The Western world has long been associated with

freedom of religion and respect for religious diversity. However, in recent years there has been a concerning rise in Christian persecution across many Western countries. While Christians are not the only religious group facing persecution, their experiences in the West are often overlooked or downplayed. This trend has many Christians worried about their safety and the ability to freely practice their faith in the future.

Persecution takes many forms, from discrimination and harassment to violence and even death. In the West, persecution against Christians often manifests in more subtle ways, such as social exclusion or the erosion of religious freedoms. For example, in some European countries it has become increasingly difficult for Christians to express their faith in public spaces by wearing religious symbols or holding public prayer meetings. In other cases, Christian business owners have faced legal action for refusing to participate in events that violate their religious beliefs.

One of the most concerning aspects of this rise in persecution is that it often goes unacknowledged by those in power. Some politicians and public figures have even actively sought to silence or demonize Christians, accusing them of being bigoted or intolerant for their religious beliefs. This has led to a culture of fear and intimidation, leaving many Christians feeling as though they must keep their faith hidden or risk being ostracized from society.

It is worth noting that the rise in Christian persecution is not limited to the Western world. Christians face persecution and violence in many countries around the world, often at the hands of oppressive regimes or extremist groups. However, the fact that this trend is also being seen in the Western world, where religious freedom is supposed to be a fundamental right, is particularly concerning.

There is no easy solution to the problem of Christian persecution in the West, but it is clear that more needs to be done to address this issue. Governments must work to protect the religious freedoms of all citizens, regardless of their beliefs. This includes protecting the right of Christian business owners and public servants to act in accordance with their faith, as well as ensuring that Christians are able to express their faith freely in public spaces.

In addition, there is a need for greater public awareness and education about the issue of Christian persecution in the West. By shining a light on this problem and speaking out against it, we can help to create a culture of freedom and respect for religious diversity.

BE SET APART FROM THE WORLD

The concept of being set apart is a common theme in the Bible, especially in the New Testament. It is often associated with the idea of holiness. Christians are called to be set apart from the world and its values, and to live lives that reflect the character and teachings of Jesus Christ.

One of the best-known passages that speaks to the idea of being set apart is 1 Peter 2:9, which says, "But you are a chosen people, a royal priesthood, a holy nation, God's special possession, that you may declare the praises of him who called you out of darkness into his wonderful light." This verse describes believers as a unique and separate people whom God has chosen to serve Him and proclaim His goodness.

Similarly, in Romans 12:2, Paul urges Christians not to conform to the patterns of this world but to be transformed by the renewing of their minds. This suggests that Christians should be different from the world in their attitudes and behaviors and their thinking should be shaped by God's Word.

Other verses that speak to this theme include 2 Corinthians 6:17, which says, "Therefore, 'Come out from them and be separate, says the Lord. Touch no unclean thing, and I will receive you,'" and James 4:4, which warns believers against friendship with the world, saying, "You adulterous people, don't you know that friendship with the world means enmity against God? Therefore, anyone who chooses to be a friend of the world becomes an enemy of God."

God is calling His people out from among this worldly system—and from worldly "Christians" as well. Not everyone will receive this message, but it is for those with ears to hear and eyes to see. We can't expect everyone to see what we see. Many will continue in their rebellion. They will continue to make excuses and keep their heads buried in the sand. We must not look to these people for affirmation. We must make our own moves and return to God's perfect will for our lives. We cannot control anyone else, but we can take responsibility for our own actions.

> I hate, I despise your feasts, and I take no delight in your solemn assemblies. Even though you offer me your burnt offerings and grain offerings, I will not accept them; and the peace offerings of your fattened animals, I will not look upon them. Take away from me the noise of your songs; to the melody of your harps I will not listen. But let justice roll down like waters, and righteousness like an ever-flowing stream.
> —Amos 5:21–24, esv

In the Book of Amos, God expresses His displeasure with the offerings of the Jewish people. This is because the people were performing religious rituals and sacrifices without truly understanding the purpose behind them. They were going through the motions of offering sacrifices, but their hearts were not in the right place.

The New International Version translation of Amos 5:21–24 says, "I hate, I despise your religious festivals; your assemblies are a stench to me. Even though you bring me burnt offerings and grain offerings, I will not accept them....But let justice roll on like a river, righteousness like a never-failing stream!" This passage shows that God is less concerned with the outward appearance of religious rituals and more concerned with the inner attitudes and actions of His people.

God desires that His people not only offer sacrifices but also live justly and righteously. This means treating others with love and compassion, seeking justice for the oppressed, and living according to God's commandments. The Jewish people had failed to do these things, so their offerings were not pleasing to God.

God did not hate the offerings the Jews were bringing. Instead, He was displeased that they were performing religious rituals without truly understanding the significance behind them and without living out the values of justice and righteousness that these rituals were meant to inspire. One thing that absolutely cannot be faked is the anointing of the Holy Spirit! We may be able to put on a show for a while, but eventually what has been done in darkness will be brought to light.

The prophet Amos lived in the eighth century BC and was sent by God to prophesy to the people of Israel, warning them of the judgment that would come due to their sin and disobedience. The Book of Amos records the messages that he delivered, including the declaration of destruction upon Israel and the promise of restoration.

God declared that He would bring destruction upon Israel because of their disobedience and sin. The people had turned away from God and started to worship idols and engage in other sinful practices. They had also become wealthy and prosperous, but their wealth was gained through exploitation and injustice, leading to great social inequality and the oppression of the poor.

Through His prophet Amos, God declared that He would punish the people for their sins by sending famine, drought, and other disasters to the land. He warned that the people's wealth and power would not save them from the coming judgment and that the nation would be destroyed.

However, even in the midst of His warning of judgment, God also promised to restore His people. He declared that after the destruction, He would rebuild the nation and restore it to its former glory. This restoration would be based on justice and righteousness rather than exploitation and oppression. God promised that He would bless the people and make them a great and prosperous nation once again.

> For behold, I will command, and shake the house
> of Israel among all the nations as one shakes with
> a sieve, but no pebble shall fall to the earth. All the
> sinners of my people shall die by the sword, who say,
> "Disaster shall not overtake or meet us."
> —AMOS 9:9–10, ESV

This is so important for us to understand! A sieve is a tool that is used to separate the coarser particles of a substance from the finer ones. In the spirit realm, God will often use persecution or suffering to shake the people who claim His name.[1] When faced with severe persecution, if a person doesn't have the Holy Spirit, he or she will not be able to stand. It's that simple. In the words of blogger Brittany Lee Allen, "They will be like the finer particles that slip through the tiny holes, not having the wholeness needed to remain in the sieve."[2]

No matter how hard we are shaken or how severely we are persecuted, attacked, or pressured, we must remain planted on the firm foundation, the solid rock of Jesus Christ! He is the Rock of Ages. Think about the parable of the wise and the foolish builders (Matt. 7:24–27), and make sure your house is built on the Rock.

BE BOLD

The apostle Paul is widely recognized as one of the most influential figures in the development of Christianity. He played a critical role in spreading the gospel throughout the Mediterranean world, and his writings in the New Testament continue to inspire and challenge believers today.

One of the key features of Paul's ministry was his boldness. Despite facing numerous challenges and much opposition, Paul remained steadfast in his commitment to proclaiming the gospel. In his letters, he often spoke of his desire for revival and his willingness to do whatever it takes to see people come to faith in Jesus.

For example, in his letter to the Romans, Paul writes, "I am not ashamed of the gospel, because it is the power of God that brings salvation to everyone who believes" (Rom. 1:16). This statement captures Paul's conviction that the gospel is the solution to the spiritual needs of humanity, and that it was his duty to share this message with as many people as possible.

Throughout his ministry Paul traveled extensively and preached in a wide range of contexts, from synagogues and public squares to private homes and prisons. He faced intense opposition from both religious leaders and political authorities, but he refused to back down or compromise his message.

In the Book of Acts we see numerous examples of Paul's boldness in action. For instance, in Acts 13, Paul and his companion Barnabas were confronted by a sorcerer named Elymas who tried to prevent them from sharing the gospel with a Roman proconsul. (See Acts 13:6–12.) In response, Paul confronted Elymas and rebuked him, saying: "You are a child of the devil and an enemy of everything that is right! You are full of all kinds of deceit and trickery. Will you never stop perverting the right ways of the Lord?" (Acts 13:10).

This may seem confrontational to modern readers, but it was essential to Paul's ministry. He understood that he was engaged in a spiritual battle for the hearts and minds of people and that he needed to be bold and courageous in order to make an impact.

The apostle Paul's boldness was a hallmark of his ministry. He was driven by a deep passion for revival and a commitment to sharing the gospel with as many people as possible. Despite facing significant challenges and great opposition, he refused to back down or compromise his message. As a result, Paul's legacy continues to inspire and challenge believers today, encouraging us to be bold in our own efforts to share the love of Christ with the world.

Like Paul, we as believers need to be bold. Too many Christians are afraid to speak up and live out their faith openly. God responds to those who call on Him. Again, there is no way to fake it with God. He knows and sees all.

HAVE FAITH

Though faith is a gift in and of itself, it is also what God responds to. Without faith it is impossible to please Him, but with the faith of a mustard seed He can move a mountain! When we exercise faith, God sees it as an invitation to intervene and manifest Himself in our lives in surprising ways. This is one reason I believe that those who walk in what I call "big faith" will see the biggest breakthroughs in their lives. The people who trust God the most and put their hope in Him are the same people who will endure until the end.

I have seen God do things that seemed absolutely impossible. Some of the most successful people I know are those who took the biggest risks. We are living in a time when Christians must get out of the boat and walk on water. We can't simply look to what this one or that one says, as we have to learn to hear the voice of God for ourselves.

It is my prayer that the church put its focus back on discipleship and prayer. Believers who know the Word, are prayer warriors, and are solidified in their understanding of their identity in Christ are the biggest threat to the enemy. They are the ones who walk in the anointing.

OUR GOD HAS NO LIMITS

The Bible teaches that God is limitless and infinite in His power and abilities. Therefore, it is important that we do not allow our understanding or beliefs about God to limit Him.

One way the Bible emphasizes God's limitless nature is by highlighting the many miraculous acts that He performed throughout history. For example, in the Old Testament we see God parting the Red Sea for the Israelites to cross, providing manna from heaven, and even causing the walls of Jericho to fall with only a shout. In the New Testament we see Jesus healing the sick, feeding thousands of people with just a few loaves of bread and two small fish, and even raising the dead.

Through these miraculous acts we see that God's power and abilities are beyond our human comprehension. As Isaiah 55:8–9 says, "For my thoughts are not your thoughts, neither are your ways my ways....As the heavens are higher than the earth, so are my ways higher than your ways and my thoughts than your thoughts."

However, it's not just about recognizing God's power but also having faith and trusting in Him. In Mark 11:22–24 Jesus tells His disciples, "Have faith in God... Truly I tell you, if anyone says to this mountain, 'Go, throw yourself into the sea,' and does not doubt in their heart but believes that what they say will happen, it will be done for them. Therefore I tell you, whatever you ask for in prayer, believe that you have received it, and it will be yours."

This passage emphasizes that if we have faith and trust in God, we should not limit Him by doubting what He can do in our lives. Rather, we should recognize His infinite power, trust in His abilities, and have faith that He can work miracles in our lives and in the world around us.

WHAT WILL HAPPEN TO THE CHURCH IN THE NEXT FEW YEARS AND BEYOND?

We are living in a disruptive period of time. Norms that have governed many aspects of society and our lives for years are being challenged. This is also happening in the body of Christ. I believe this shaking—the shaking of the church, at least—is God's hand at work. This needed to happen in order for the church to course-correct, among many other reasons we will discuss later. The challenge is that change is uncomfortable and overwhelming at times, especially for people who are non-confrontational or set in their ways.

Many people are deeply entrenched in religion rather than focusing on a relationship with God in which they inquire of the Holy Spirit. There is a big difference between the two. This explains the infighting among Christians we are seeing play out, especially on social media. In reality the fight is religious people and non-believers versus people who are led by the Spirit. Their ideas and worldviews are colliding. No one wants to admit he or she is wrong.

Few people are being mentored or held accountable, so we see a significant number of "Christians" who are dug in due to pride. Most of these people don't actually ask the Holy Spirit for guidance. They are not filled with the Holy Spirit, nor do they operate in the fruit of the Spirit. Yet if you were to ask them if they are Christians, they would say yes. This is because in many churches the gospel has been so watered down that people don't even know what the Bible says. It is a "wide gate" mentality. (See Matthew 7:13–14 and Luke 13:22–30.)

On the other hand, we must also be mindful of the temptation to be too free or too emotional and synchronize some of the freedom we walk in with false religions and beliefs. This often happens when people who are on the right side fall into deception and doctrines being taught by online personalities and ministers who are not tethered to the body of Christ or held accountable. I believe many people will be deceived in this way in the coming years, as I have seen it happening often in recent years.

Much of the shaking we are seeing around the world is things being set into place for what is to come. We are witnessing the Book of Revelation beginning to really take shape as key biblical prophecies are being positioned to soon manifest in the natural. It is an exciting time to be alive. I liken it to the best of times and the worst of times simultaneously. While many people are still looking for positive and hopeful messages and remain silent, the globalist agenda—which is demonically inspired—continues to advance full steam ahead with little resistance. As this is happening, the church seems to be bickering and digging in deeper on views, positions, traditions, and denominational variances rather than combining our efforts in order to effectively respond to what's taking place all around us. A house divided against itself cannot stand. I believe we are only years away from a total societal shift in the West and subsequently the world order as a whole. This will have dramatic implications for us all, including the church.

As the World Economic Forum and other globalist institutions continue to craft and initiate new policies and implement their go-forward agenda, we will begin to see large parts of biblical Christianity deemed hateful and socially unacceptable. The pressure for Christians and Christian organizations to cave and capitulate on these key issues and areas of core Christian doctrine will intensify to a level of critical mass, which is why we need to build community and surround ourselves with intercessors who will pray for us and stand with us.

As these events continue and the pressure increases, we will see different responses from the pulpit. Some pastors will quit the ministry, finding the pressure simply too intense.

Others will take what they consider to be the high road and continue to ignore the reality of the situation, much like many ministers are doing now. They will double down on speaking motivational, feel-good types of messages while ignoring what is going on in the world around them, hoping that if they simply ignore it, it will leave them alone. Unfortunately, they are dead wrong in that view.

The third group is the lions—ministers who rise to the occasion, take a stand, and fight the good fight of faith no matter the obstacles thrown in their path. I will refer to these people as "lions" throughout the remainder of this book, as the Lord showed me this is the season for lions and generals of the faith to stand up and be bold and unafraid, to die to their flesh and put on the full armor of God each day.

While many self-proclaimed prophetic voices are

claiming that things are about to get much better, we know through discernment, prayer, and biblical precedent that unless we repent and truly come out from among them, our nation will likely suffer a similar fate as the people of ancient Israel did before they turned back to God.

CHAPTER 6

RETHINKING CHURCH

BELIEVE THAT RETURNING to the foundation of our faith is important if we want to stay true to the original teachings of Jesus and the early Christian church. We must also separate ourselves from the darkness and wickedness of this hour.

Many of the ways that the West has done church in the last thirty-plus years have been a significant departure from the traditional practices and beliefs of our faith. Some of the new ways of doing church, such as megachurches, celebrity Christianity, and a focus on entertainment and consumerism, have taken away from the central message of Christianity and led to a lack of depth and sincerity in our faith. This is why the church is not having as much of an impact on the culture as we need to.

Returning to our foundation involves a renewed focus on Scripture, prayer, community, and service. It could also involve a greater emphasis on traditional practices such as regular attendance at church services, personal Bible study, and participation in small-group discussions or Bible studies. In addition, we need to reintroduce mentorship, discipleship, and accountability.

I believe that being filled with the Holy Spirit is essential because it empowers believers to live in a way that is pleasing to God and to carry out His purposes in the world. It also gives us the discernment we need to navigate the very challenging world around us. I often refer to the current spiritual environment as a minefield. We need wisdom and direction from above to help guide us as we walk through this life.

According to the Bible, the Holy Spirit is the third person of the Trinity, equal with God the Father and God the Son. When we became Christians, we received the Holy Spirit as a gift from God, and the Spirit came to live within us to guide and empower us.

Being filled with the Holy Spirit involves being continually filled with His power and presence as we yield to His guidance and direction. This filling helps us to live in obedience to God's will, to resist temptation and sin, and to live a life of love and service to others.

The Bible also teaches that being filled with the Holy Spirit brings about transformation in our lives along with spiritual fruit such as love, joy, peace, patience, kindness, goodness, faithfulness, gentleness, and self-control (Gal. 5:22–23, ESV). These qualities are evidence of the Holy Spirit's work in our lives, and they reflect the character of Christ.

This is why all Christians must seek to be filled with the Holy Spirit—so that we can live lives that are pleasing to God, carry out His purposes in the world, and reflect the character of Christ.

FOLLOWERS OF THE WAY

The Way is a term the Bible uses to refer to the early Christian movement. The followers of the Way were those who believed in Jesus Christ as the Messiah and followed His teachings.

The term *the Way* appears several times in the New Testament, particularly in the Book of Acts. Acts 9:2, for example, says that Saul (later known as Paul) was going to Damascus to arrest anyone who "belonged to the Way." In Acts 19:9–10 we read that Paul "took the disciples with him and had discussions daily in the lecture hall of Tyrannus. This went on for two years, so that all the Jews and Greeks who lived in the province of Asia heard the word of the Lord."

The followers of the Way were also referred to as "disciples" (Acts 6:1), "believers" (Acts 5:14, KJV), and "saints" (Rom. 1:7, KJV). They were a diverse group of people, comprised of Jews and Gentiles, men and women, and people from all walks of life.

The followers of the Way were persecuted for their beliefs, particularly by the Jewish authorities and the Roman Empire. However, their faith continued to spread, and the early Christian movement eventually became the dominant religion of the Roman Empire.

Today there are various Bibles that include "the Way"

in their titles. I mention this at the beginning of this chapter because I believe God is taking us back to our roots, to the foundations of our faith. In studying the beginnings of the church, we must understand where we came from in order to know who we truly are as believers. Right now, God is allowing a shaking to take place in the body of Christ so that we will turn back to Him and rid ourselves of religious beliefs like those of the Pharisees, which are not in line with Scripture or from the Lord at all.

RELIGION VERSUS RELATIONSHIP

Religious rituals and practices can be an important part of our faith and can provide a meaningful way to express our beliefs and connection with the divine. However, it's important to understand that not all religious rituals are compatible with true faith in Jesus Christ.

In Christianity, faith in Jesus is centered on a personal relationship with Him as the Son of God and Savior of humanity. The Bible teaches that salvation comes through faith in Jesus alone, not through adherence to religious rituals or traditions.

When people mix old religious rituals with faith in Jesus, they risk diluting the central message of Christianity and potentially contradicting or obscuring its essential teachings. This can lead to confusion and a distorted understanding of the faith, which can ultimately hinder spiritual growth and the development of a deeper relationship with God.

Furthermore, some old religious rituals involve practices or beliefs that are incompatible with Christianity. For example, some rituals involve the worship of other deities or the use of divination or other spiritual practices that are not consistent with the teachings of the Bible. In many cases there is idolatry involved.

While some rituals can be an important part of our faith, we must ensure that everything we do is consistent with the teachings of Jesus and the Bible to avoid compromising the core principles of our faith and the Word of God.

In many ways that are worth noting, religion is much different from having a true relationship with God. Religion refers to a set of beliefs, rituals, practices, and traditions that are typically organized around a specific deity or deities. It can involve a structured system of beliefs and practices as well as adherence to religious rules and regulations. Religion often includes a hierarchy of religious leaders who guide and interpret religious teachings.

On the other hand, a true relationship with God involves a personal and intimate connection between an individual and God. It involves a sense of spiritual connection and a desire to live in obedience to God. The Lord said, "If you love Me, keep My commandments" (John 14:15, NKJV). A relationship with God is often marked by feelings of love, peace, and joy.

While religion can provide a framework for understanding and connecting with God, it is not always necessary for a true relationship with God. It is possible for someone to develop a personal connection with God through consistent prayer, worship, and getting into God's Word regularly without adhering to a specific religious tradition. Similarly, an individual can practice a religion without necessarily having a personal relationship with God.

We must learn to recognize the difference between participating in religion and having a true relationship with the living God. There is a distinct difference between the two that determines whether we will grow in our faith or simply check a box.

WARNING ABOUT EXTREME GRACE AND HYPER-GRACE

Even though God gives us much grace, we still need to be a repentant people and do all that we can to live in a way that pleases the Lord. In the last thirty years, the hyper-grace movement has done much damage to the church as a whole. Those who preach it have taken God's grace out of context and used it to tickle ears and push a very watered-down version of Christianity.

While God does give us extreme grace and mercy, we can't take advantage of it. Romans 6:23 tells us the wages of sin is death, and when you open a door of sin in your life, the enemy will use it against you and cause major issues, afflictions, and challenges that could have otherwise been avoided. In other words, sin has consequences. Even though God will forgive us when we truly repent, this doesn't mean we won't have to deal with the repercussions of our actions. This is why we are much better off simply obeying what God tells us in His Word and not opening these doors in our lives.

This is why Paul so urgently warned us, "Do not give place to the devil" (Eph. 4:27, MEV). In other words, we must stay on alert to keep the enemy from freely accessing our lives. Believe me, the devil will loiter around to see if you are serious about keeping him out of your life.

I saw this happen when I left Hollywood many years ago. The enemy literally rolled out the red carpet for me and tried to entice me to go back to my worldly ways. It was like everything I had ever wanted was suddenly being presented to me. He will do this anytime we give him the opportunity.

This reminds me of when Satan tempted Jesus in the wilderness. How did Jesus respond? He said, "It is written," and told the devil to get behind Him! (See Matthew 4:1–11.) We should respond in a similar way when the devil comes to tempt us. Thank God, I was able to ask the Lord for strength as a new believer, and I truly walked away from my past for good, even when tempted with extreme worldly favor and what appeared to be great opportunities. We must remember that God is always good, but not everything that looks good is of God.

NO OPEN DOORS TO SIN

The Bible teaches that sin is a destructive force that can have serious consequences in our lives. Sin is defined as an act of disobedience against God and can manifest in various forms such as lying, cheating, stealing, and sexual immorality. In the Book of James it is written that sin, when fully grown, brings forth death (Jas. 1:15). This is why the Bible admonishes us to leave no open doors to sin in our lives.

The concept of leaving no doors open to sin is rooted in the belief that as humans, we are prone to temptation and can easily fall into sin if we are not careful. The apostle Paul wrote in his letter to the Corinthians, "No temptation has overtaken you except what is common to mankind. And God is faithful; he will not let you be tempted beyond what you can bear. But when you are tempted, he will also provide a way out so that you can endure it" (1 Cor. 10:13).

This passage underscores the fact that we can resist temptation and overcome sin if we rely on God's strength and power. However, we must also take responsibility for our actions and be proactive by avoiding situations that could lead us into sin. This involves being mindful of our thoughts, actions, and associations and avoiding anything that could compromise our faith and integrity.

Proverbs 4:23 says, "Above all else, guard your heart, for everything you do flows from it." This verse teaches us that the heart is the wellspring of life, and if we allow sin to take root in our hearts, it will eventually manifest in our actions and behavior. Therefore, we must be vigilant and guard our hearts against the influences of the world that could lead us astray.

Leaving no open doors to sin also means being intentional about living a life that is pleasing to God. This involves making conscious decisions to honor God in all that we do and resisting the temptation to compromise our faith for the sake of convenience or worldly pleasures. The apostle Paul exhorts us to "present [our] bodies as a living sacrifice, holy and pleasing to God" (Rom. 12:1).

In order to leave no open doors to sin, we must avoid situations that could compromise our faith and integrity, guard our hearts against the influences of the world, and be intentional about living lives that are pleasing to God. By relying on God's strength and power, we can overcome temptation and walk in righteousness, and as the Book of Proverbs says, "The path of the righteous is like the morning sun, shining ever brighter till the full light of day" (Prov. 4:18).

This is one way that we must come out from among them. We must be unwilling to compromise, and instead live with the favor and blessing of Jesus Christ!

CHAPTER 7

BACK TO BASICS AND RESTORING THE FOUNDATIONS

I STRONGLY BELIEVE THAT God wants to restore the foundations of the church and subsequently our nation. There has been a massive effort to rewrite history and negate the fact that America was founded on Christian principles. However, we know that our founders believed in "life, liberty, and the pursuit of happiness," and that these rights were given to us by God and not by the government. They referred to these as "certain unalienable rights" and crafted our Declaration of Independence and our Constitution based on this Judeo-Christian viewpoint.

Several members of the Continental Congress were pastors or strong Christian believers who would openly pray and speak about their faith without restriction or censorship. There was no push for "separation of church and state" like there is now. (We will discuss this in depth below.) It is very important for Americans to understand that our Founding Fathers never intended for people of faith to stay away from or out of the government's business.

The church has been quite absent for many years when it comes to getting involved politically, which is why there has been a lack of Christian leadership in our nation and government. The church must actively engage in politics once again just as it is meant to do in all areas of society. Pastors, too, need to speak up and not hold back in this area. They cannot be hand-cuffed by worrying about losing their tax-exempt status. President Trump did what he could to lessen this burden on pastors by encouraging them and signing an executive order rolling back some of the restrictions issued during the Johnson era regarding 501(c)(3) organizations. Ultimately, pastors need to speak on all spiritual matters whether they are deemed political or not.

I have been hearing a lot of talk about revival, which I believe is a good thing. We are even seeing what I refer to as pockets of revival emerging throughout the country right now. Remnant believers have a yearning in their hearts to see a powerful move of God because we know He is the only hope and answer for this country and the world. While we want to see godly politicians and people who care about religious liberty and freedom put into positions of leadership around the nation, we also understand that no politician can save this country, only a major move of God and a return to biblical morality and values. We must apply the Bible's recipe for revival:

> If My people who are called by My name will
> humble themselves, and pray and seek My face,
> and turn from their wicked ways, then I will hear
> from heaven, and will forgive their sin and heal
> their land.
>
> —2 CHRONICLES 7:14, NKJV

God has given me some key words regarding how we can restore our foundations and return to God. If the church as a whole does this, it will be a game changer and pave the way for true revival to take place. Remember the Lord says, "If My people." He wants the church to consecrate itself and return to Him, to get away from the traditions of man and back to the basics and fundamentals of our faith.

Here is a list of some key words God has put on my heart and the main areas that need to be restored:

1. **Souls**: We must return to the Great Commission and tend to the harvest.

2. **Harvest**: We need laborers with hearts for the harvest and a new generation of evangelists.

3. **Truth**: We need to speak the truth boldly and push back against the demonic false narratives.

4. Bible: The Bible has to be taught, studied, and made a priority once again.

5. Big faith and action: Faith without works is dead. We need to have strong, unwavering faith.

6. Discipleship: We must take the time to disciple and mentor people. We are severely lacking in this area right now, as many people are so hungry and looking for an elder to mentor them.

7. Kingdom business: Instead of building our own kingdoms, we need to focus on building God's kingdom and work together for the glory of God. This is not about us; it's about *Him*!

8. Kingdom-minded: We have to pray and ask the Lord for His heart and for divine wisdom and strategy. He will show us what we need to do.

9. The anointing of the Holy Spirit: We must operate in the anointing of the Holy Spirit. This requires us to have an active prayer life and seek the heart of the Father each day. It is the anointing that breaks the yoke of bondage.

10. **Wisdom**: We need wisdom from above. We must pray and even fast over certain matters to receive breakthrough and hear from the Lord clearly.

11. **Discernment**: To avoid the deceptions of this hour, we must constantly inquire of the Lord and be led by His Spirit. We also must test the spirits, as there is much deception in the world right now.

12. **Accountability**: Pastors and other fivefold ministry leaders must be held accountable to others so they remain teachable and avoid open doors to sin.

13. **Sound doctrine**: In order to have sound doctrine, people need to know and teach the Bible. This requires study time and true teachers who are willing to teach in depth. Also, all believers need to study and get into the Word for themselves each week instead of only relying on others to teach them.

14. **Favor**: Those who are willing to consecrate, make it about souls and the harvest,

and go all in will walk in the favor and blessing of the Lord.

15. **Pure streams**: We must find and align with others who are "pure streams," people who don't have a motive or agenda but rather hunger and desire to see God move and are humble about His business.

GOING BACK TO THE BASICS

In today's world it is easy to get caught up in the hustle and bustle of life and lose sight of what really matters. As Christians, it is crucial that we take time to return to the basics and foundations of our faith. This means focusing on the core principles and values that Jesus taught us and reorienting our lives around them. Here are some reasons why it is so important that we do so.

First and foremost, returning to the basics of our faith will help us deepen our relationship with God. When we are focused on the essentials, we are better able to connect with God on a spiritual level. We are more attuned to His presence in our lives, and we are more likely to hear His voice and receive His guidance. This in turn can bring us a sense of peace and fulfillment that we cannot find elsewhere.

Another reason why it is important to return to the basics is that it helps us to stay grounded in our faith. In a world that is constantly changing and evolving, it can be difficult to know what to believe or how to live our lives. By returning to the foundational principles of Christianity, we can be sure that we are following a solid and reliable path, which will give us a sense of stability and security in an uncertain world.

Returning to the basics of our faith will also help us to be better witnesses to those around us. When we are living out the core values of Christianity, we reflect God's love and grace to the world. People are more likely to be drawn to our message when they see we are living it out in our own lives. If we return to the basics, we will be more effective ambassadors for Christ and better able to share His message with others.

Returning to the basics and foundations of our faith is essential if we want to deepen our relationship with God, stay grounded in our faith, and be effective witnesses to the world. It is easy to get distracted by the many things vying for our attention, so we must make a conscious effort to focus on what really matters. Let us take time to reflect on the core principles and values of Christianity and reorient our lives around them. May we be transformed by the renewing of our minds, and may our lives be a testimony to the goodness and grace of God.

RELIGIOUS LIBERTY AND FREEDOM

Religious persecution has been a contentious issue throughout history, and the Founding Fathers of the United States were no strangers to it. Many of them had experienced persecution firsthand, either in Europe or in the colonies, and this shaped their views on the role of religion in society and government. In this section, we will explore how the Founding Fathers of the United States dealt with religious persecution and how their beliefs shaped the founding principles of the country.

The Founding Fathers were well aware of the dangers of religious persecution, having witnessed its devastating effects on the Old World. They saw firsthand how religion could be used as a tool of oppression, with those in power using it to justify the persecution of those who held different beliefs. This experience informed their views on the role of religion in government and the importance of protecting religious freedom.

One of the earliest examples of religious persecution in the colonies was the Puritan persecution of Quakers in the Massachusetts Bay Colony in the seventeenth century. Quakers were seen as a threat to the established order, and their refusal to conform to the Puritan way of life led to their persecution. The Founding Fathers, many of whom were descended from the Puritans, were well aware of this history and were determined to prevent such persecution from happening in the new nation.

The Founding Fathers believed that the government had no right to interfere with an individual's religious beliefs or practices. They believed that everyone had the right to worship as they saw fit, without fear of persecution or discrimination. This belief was enshrined in the First Amendment to the United States Constitution, which states that "Congress shall make no law respecting an establishment of religion, or prohibiting the free exercise thereof."[1]

This principle of religious freedom was one of the defining characteristics of the United States and set it apart from many other nations at the time. The Founding Fathers understood that religious freedom was essential to the survival of a democratic society, and they were willing to fight for it.

One of the most famous examples of religious persecution in the United States was the Salem witch trials, which took place in Massachusetts in the late seventeenth century. The trials resulted in the execution of twenty people and the imprisonment of many others.[2] The Founding Fathers were deeply disturbed by these events and saw them as a warning of the dangers of religious fanaticism.

Thomas Jefferson, one of the most influential Founding Fathers, was a strong advocate of religious freedom. In his *Notes on the State of Virginia* he argued that "the legitimate powers of government extend to such acts only as are injurious to others. But it does me no injury for my neighbor to say there are twenty gods, or no god. It neither picks my pocket nor breaks my leg."[3] Jefferson believed that the government had no business interfering in matters of religion and that individuals had the right to worship as they saw fit.

James Madison, another influential Founding Father,

was also a strong advocate of religious freedom. In his famous "Memorial and Remonstrance Against Religious Assessments" he argued that the government should not be allowed to support any particular religion. He wrote, "Who does not see that the same authority which can establish Christianity, in exclusion of all other Religions, may establish with the same ease any particular sect of Christians, in exclusion of all other Sects?"[4]

The Founding Fathers' commitment to religious freedom was not without its challenges. Some believed the government should play a role in promoting and supporting a particular religion, and some saw religious minorities as a threat to the established order. However, the Founding Fathers remained committed to their principles and worked tirelessly to ensure that religious freedom was protected.

The Founding Fathers of the United States were deeply committed to protecting religious freedom and preventing religious persecution. They recognized the dangers of religious fanaticism and believed the government had no right to infringe upon the God-given inalienable rights of life, liberty, and the pursuit of happiness. They believed these rights were given to us by God and not by the government.

JEFFERSON AND THE DANBURY BAPTISTS

Thomas Jefferson, one of the Founding Fathers of the United States of America, is known for many things, including his role in drafting the Declaration of Independence, serving as the third president of the United States, and his contributions to the fields of politics, law, and philosophy. However, one of his lesser-known legacies is his involvement in the Danbury Baptist letter, which has had a significant impact on the interpretation of the First Amendment of the United States Constitution.

In 1801 the Danbury Baptist Association, a group of Baptists in Connecticut, sent a letter to President Jefferson expressing their concern about the potential infringement of their religious freedom by the government. At the time, the state of Connecticut had an established church, the Congregational Church, and the Danbury Baptists were concerned that the government might try to establish a similar church at the national level, which could threaten their freedom of worship.

In response to their letter, Jefferson wrote a now-famous letter to the Danbury Baptists in January 1802, in which he reassured them of their religious freedom and outlined his interpretation of the First Amendment of the United States Constitution. In the letter, Jefferson wrote that the First Amendment created "a wall of separation between church and state" and that this was a fundamental principle of the American government.[5]

The concept of separation of church and state had been discussed by earlier thinkers, including John Locke,[6] but Jefferson's letter to the Danbury Baptists popularized the phrase and made it a cornerstone of American constitutional law. The idea behind separation of church and state is that the government should not promote or favor any particular religion or religious institution and individuals should be free to practice their religion—or no religion at all—without fear of persecution or discrimination.

The phrase "wall of separation between church and state" has been the subject of much debate and interpretation over the years. Some have argued that it means that religion has no place in government and that religious beliefs should not influence public policy; however, that was not Jefferson's argument at all. Others have argued that it simply means that the government should stay out of the church's business.

Regardless of the interpretation, Jefferson's letter to the Danbury Baptists has had a profound impact on the interpretation of the First Amendment and American constitutional law more broadly. The letter has been cited in numerous court cases over the years, including in the landmark Supreme Court case of Everson v. Board of Education in 1947, in which the Court ruled that the Establishment Clause of the First Amendment applied to the states and prohibited them from using public funds to support religious schools.

In addition to its legal significance, Jefferson's letter to the Danbury Baptists is also important for what it tells us about Jefferson's views on religion and government.

Jefferson was a strong advocate for religious freedom and believed that the government should not interfere with individuals' religious beliefs or practices.

Thomas Jefferson's letter to the Danbury Baptists is an important document in American history, both for its legal significance and for what it tells us about Jefferson's views on religion and government. All Christians need to understand the importance of religious freedom and the need to keep the government out of the church's business. We saw this greatly infringed upon during COVID-19. Churches in many places were forced to shut down for a period of time. This can never be allowed to happen again, as it goes against our First Amendment rights. I am so thankful for those pastors who stood during this time. They are the lions and generals we so often talk about.

THE PRESENT BATTLE FOR RELIGIOUS LIBERTY AND FREEDOM

Religious liberty has been a hotly debated issue in the United States for many years. Recently, several high-profile cases have sparked intense public discussion about the boundaries of religious freedom. From the refusal to bake a cake for a same-sex wedding to the right of pharmacists to refuse to fill prescriptions for contraceptives, these cases have raised complex legal and ethical questions about the intersection of religious belief and individual rights.

One of the most well-known religious liberty cases in recent years was Masterpiece Cakeshop, Ltd. v. Colorado Civil Rights Commission. In this 2018 case, the owner of a Colorado bakery declined to prepare a wedding cake for a same-sex couple because of his religious beliefs. The couple filed a complaint with the Colorado Civil Rights Commission, which ruled that the bakery had violated state anti-discrimination laws. The case eventually made its way to the Supreme Court, which narrowly ruled in favor of the bakery, citing the commission's hostility toward the owner's religious beliefs.[7]

Another notable case is Fulton v. City of Philadelphia, which was decided by the Supreme Court in 2021. In this case, a Catholic foster care agency in Philadelphia refused to work with same-sex couples, citing its religious beliefs. The city then refused to renew the agency's contract, arguing that it was violating the city's anti-discrimination policy. The Supreme Court ruled in favor of the agency, finding that the city's policy was not neutral and was therefore a violation of the agency's religious liberty.[8]

In addition to these cases, there have been a number of recent religious liberty cases involving health-care providers. For example, in Stormans v. Wiesman, a group of pharmacists in Washington State refused to fill prescriptions for emergency contraceptives, citing their religious beliefs. The state pharmacy board eventually issued a rule requiring pharmacies to stock and dispense all legally prescribed drugs, including contraceptives.[9] The case was appealed to the Supreme Court, which declined to hear it.

Similarly, in Little Sisters of the Poor Saints Peter and Paul Home v. Pennsylvania, a group of Catholic nuns challenged the Affordable Care Act's requirement that employers provide contraception coverage to their employees. The case was eventually heard by the Supreme Court, which ruled in favor of the nuns, finding that the government had not adequately considered less restrictive alternatives to the contraceptive mandate.[10]

These cases and others like them raise important questions about the balance between religious liberty and other individual rights, such as the right to be free from discrimination. Supporters of religious liberty argue that individuals and organizations should be able to exercise their religious beliefs without fear of retribution or discrimination. They argue that the government should not be able to force individuals to violate their religious beliefs as a condition of participating in public life.

According to an article in *Touchstone*, "The present struggle over religious freedom boils down to two sides. The first are those who believe they have a fundamental right, protected by the First Amendment, to practice their faith freely and openly in society."[11] (For this reason, we started the Religious Liberty Coalition, which is designed to stand up for religious liberties and circles the wagons around those who come under attack in the area. You can find out more about this by going to www.RLCUS.org.)

We recently saw a man get raided and subsequently arrested for doing just that. Only a decade ago, arresting someone simply for practicing his religion would have been considered taboo in America, but as religious liberties and rights are continually being eroded, we are seeing cases like this become more and more common.

LET'S KEEP FIGHTING AND STANDING

Religious liberty and freedom are fundamental values in many societies, including the United States. The First Amendment of the US Constitution explicitly protects the freedom of religion, which includes the right to exercise one's religion, as well as the right to be free from government interference in matters of religion.

From a Christian perspective, religious liberty and freedom are important because they allow individuals and communities to freely practice and express their faith. This includes the right to worship, evangelize, and engage in religious education and charitable activities without fear of government persecution or interference.

Furthermore, as Christians we believe that our faith is not just a private matter, but it also shapes our public actions and engagement with the wider world. As such, the protection of religious liberty and freedom is essential to maintaining Christians' ability to participate fully in public life and promote their values and beliefs.

We also feel that our religious liberties are being threatened in certain contexts. For example, we object to government mandates that conflict with our religious beliefs, such as requirements to provide contraception or perform same-sex marriages. In these cases, we feel that our religious liberty is being infringed upon and that we have a right to resist or challenge these mandates.

Overall, the protection of religious liberty and freedom is valued by many Christians as well as people of other faiths and even secularists. It is important for governments and societies to ensure that these rights are protected and upheld so that individuals and communities are free to practice and express their beliefs without fear of persecution or interference.

CHAPTER 8

OUR IDENTITY IN CHRIST

DON'T COMPARE YOURSELF to others. Most of the people who are out there making it look like their lives are so glamorous, perfect, and special online are only showing the images they want us to see. They are putting their best selfies up, all touched up and perfect, yet we don't see the rest. We only see an image. We see only what they want us to. We need to be mindful of this and avoid the pressure to compare ourselves to others.

I guarantee you this: The people you see online have problems, flaws, and real challenges just like we all do! Some people just work hard to hide it. Some people make a living off an image. If there is one thing I can tell you after twenty years of counseling people and having grown up in Hollywood—two unique perspectives—it's this: Things are not as they appear! Not even close. Some of the celebrities that I know personally are the most broken and insecure people I have ever met.

Life is a blessing, but it is a series of ups and downs. We all face many high highs and many low lows, mountaintop and valley experiences. What counts is how we respond and react in each season. The key is where we look, whom and what we look to, and from where we draw our strength, especially in pivotal moments of decision.

If we are in Christ, we draw our strength from Him! He gets us through it all. He is always faithful. He is real. He is authentic. He is love. He is enough! He gives us what we need to be set up for real success—eternal success! He is our very present help in times of need. He knows and sees all. He always gives us a way out. He always makes a way, even when it seems like there is no way.

Life is not about likes, followers, views, money, fame, fortune, or clicks. We cannot take any of that to heaven. One day we will stand before the throne of glory. That's what it's all about: souls. Our soul, winning souls! Not my ministry, or your ministry—it's all *God's* ministry! He gives and takes away. Don't look at me; look at Him!

To put things in perspective, you can have a million followers and not save one soul. You can have twelve followers and change the world. You can please an audience of millions with a great performance and still end up in hell. Yet if you live for an audience of One—*the* One—you will go to heaven!

By the way, I feel led to mention here that you are not the only person who ever went through a divorce, or was cheated on, or was physically abused, or had an abortion, or was addicted to drugs and alcohol, or had someone accuse you, or was molested, or was told you would never make it in life, or was angry. Maybe right now you are lonely, hurt, depressed, down on life, and want to give up. Maybe you have a bad self-image. This is all understandable. I get it.

There are so many people dealing with the same things you are. Are you struggling with a tough marriage or a difficult financial situation? No matter what your issue may be, God sees and understands everything you are going through. You are not alone in this. He is with you.

I know it's hard living in this world of smoke and mirrors where everything seems upside down and inside out, where good is called evil and evil is called good. This culture is constantly trying to allure us, cause us to compare ourselves to others or to engage in sin—which is literally everywhere! This is all a distraction.

You are not less than others. You are no less special to God than anyone else. The devil has been lying to you and attempting to rob you of your joy. This is what he does. Do not allow him to! You were fearfully and wonderfully made. Your life has a purpose!

I strongly felt led to put this in here. This is my message to the person out there who is really struggling: Please realize how important your life is and know that God does hear your prayers! I believe a breakthrough is on its way for you—probably a lot sooner than you realize.

Keep praying. Keep standing. Know your identity in Christ. Never give up—never. You are beautiful, special, and greatly loved by the Lord. Don't compare yourself to others, as not one of them could ever be you. There is only one of you! Instead of comparing ourselves to others, let's all strive to be more like Jesus. Now, that is wisdom!

CONFIDENCE IN CHRIST

For Christians, having confidence in their identity in Christ is essential to living a fulfilling and purposeful life. The concept of identity in Christ is rooted in the belief that individuals were created in God's image and that their true identity is found in their relationship with Jesus Christ. We will now explore why it is important for Christians to have confidence in their identity in Christ and the benefits that come with it.

Identity in Christ provides a sense of purpose.

One significant benefit of having confidence in your identity in Christ is that it provides a sense of purpose. As a Christian, your identity is rooted in your relationship with Christ, and this relationship should motivate and guide your decisions and actions. When you have a deep understanding of your identity in Christ, you are better able to understand your purpose and calling in life. You can confidently pursue your passions and interests, knowing that they are aligned with God's plan for your life.

Identity in Christ helps combat insecurity.

Another benefit of having confidence in your identity in Christ is that it helps combat insecurity. In a world where many people base their worth on external factors such as appearance, status, and material possessions, it is easy to fall into the trap of feeling insecure. However, when you have a deep understanding of your identity in Christ, you can find security and confidence in the fact that your worth and value are based not on external factors but rather on the love and grace of God.

Identity in Christ brings freedom.

Having confidence in your identity in Christ also brings freedom. When you have a deep understanding of your identity in Christ, you are freed from the pressure to conform to societal standards and expectations. You are free to be yourself and pursue your unique calling, knowing that your worth and value are not based on what others think of you but on your relationship with Christ.

Identity in Christ helps build healthy relationships.

Having confidence in your identity in Christ is also crucial for building healthy relationships. When you have a deep understanding of your identity in Christ, you are less likely to seek validation and acceptance from others. Instead, you can enter into relationships with a healthy sense of self-worth and confidence, which can help you build deeper, more meaningful connections with others.

Identity in Christ provides a strong foundation for life.

Having confidence in your identity in Christ provides a strong foundation for life. When you know who you are in Christ, you can navigate life's challenges with confidence and resilience. You can trust that God is in control and that He has a plan and a purpose for your life, even when things don't go as planned. This can provide a sense of peace and security that is hard to find in the world.

Having confidence in your identity in Christ is crucial for living a fulfilling and purposeful life. It provides a sense of purpose, helps combat insecurity, brings freedom, helps build healthy relationships, and provides a strong foundation for life. As Christians, we should strive to deepen our understanding of our identity in Christ and allow it to guide our decisions and actions.

WORDS—DON'T LET THEM DEFINE YOU!

I want to speak about something that I have seen for many years in counseling people and that afflicts the lives of so many people. I have walked through this personally and even broken some words that were once spoken over me—now I am healed of them! I understand. Trust me, this works!

What am I talking about? I am talking about the words that people have spoken over you and me, things that were said to us throughout our lives (often when we were kids) that were simply untrue. Sometimes even if we know they weren't true, those words have still taken root in our hearts.

This happens often, even to believers. We tend to carry these words along with us as excess baggage throughout our lives until we deal with them. Sometimes we begin to believe what was said (even if it wasn't true) and take it on as part of our identity and persona. We cannot do this! We need to learn who we are in Jesus Christ! He tells us, "If the Son sets you free, you will be free indeed" (John 8:36)!

Words are powerful. In fact, the Bible says that "death and life are in the power of the tongue" (Prov. 18:21, NKJV). This means that when a person speaks a curse, death, false words, or lies over you or about you (or me), they can indeed affect your life and situation. Sometimes people hook into them so strongly that it leads to their ultimate demise. They bought into the lie that was spoken over them, and the lie ended up being their downfall. That is what the enemy wants, but we say "No!" in the name of Jesus. This will not be our fate!

HOW WE CAN HAVE COMPLETE VICTORY

God has given us all the tools we need to be set up for ultimate success here on earth. He also has given us authority in the name of Jesus to break every curse, lie, and false word that has been spoken over us. We can go before the Lord and ask Him to heal our hearts and let us see the truth through wisdom and discernment. We can pray, "Lord, give me ears to hear and eyes to see the truth." We can learn to see ourselves as God sees us! We can study His Word and learn how to fight in the Spirit over these matters! Once we do, that's it. It's done! Those words will no longer have authority over our lives. They are forever canceled!

God said in His Word that He made us "fearfully and wonderfully" (Ps. 139:14). He also said He made us in His likeness and "His own image" (Gen. 1:27, NKJV). He knows the plans He has for you, "plans to prosper you and not to harm you, plans to give you hope and a future" (Jer. 29:11). His promises are yes and amen. We are in the world but not of the world. We are citizens of heaven! Thank God that He is the author and finisher of our story!

In most cases, the people who spoke negatively about us spoke out of their own brokenness, hurt, and woundedness. What they said was never the truth. That's why we simply break those words and the spirit behind them, cast them down, and move forward in victory. We bind them, as the Bible instructs us to do.

Sometimes it is not even the person who is saying those hurtful words but rather a demon speaking through them! This is a common way the demonic realm attacks Christians. Our battle is not against flesh and blood but rather against strongholds and principalities. The good news is that we can win and beat back the enemy, his demonic minions, and all his attacks each and every time! "The gates of hell shall not prevail" (Matt. 16:18, ESV)! "Greater is He that is in you, than he that is in the world" (1 John 4:4, KJV). God is our defense!

I wanted to share this with you today because I know how it feels when someone speaks death over your life and situation. I've had to learn how to overcome what people have said to me or spoken over me. I could have believed them and never been able to accomplish what God has called me to do, but instead someone once shared with me what I am sharing with you today, and I learned the truth. They told me who I am in Jesus Christ. They told me I can walk in the authority and anointing of the Holy Spirit! They shared how believers have complete victory in Jesus Christ. Yes we do! Once I embraced this reality, God moved in my life so powerfully that it's truly amazing—and He will do the same for you!

We are built to overcome. We must simply know who we are in Jesus Christ and walk in that reality. He is our foundation. He is our refuge. He loves us so much—and He made us! God doesn't make any mistakes! You are special and unique, and there is no other person on this planet that can be you. Period. Only you can be you! And you have a calling and a purpose that is unique to you as well.

Let's all step into that calling today, if you haven't already, and see all God has in store for our lives! We can thrive even when the world is going crazy!

Today we break all negative words and lies from the

pit of hell over our lives. No longer will we allow these words to take root in our hearts and minds! We bind them and cast them down forever in Jesus' name. It is done. It is finished!

Jesus Christ has given us complete healing and complete victory this day! Knowing who we are in Christ and walking in that authority is a huge part of coming out from among them.

CHAPTER 9

THE ANOINTING

THE ANOINTING OF the Holy Spirit is a significant concept in the Bible. It refers to the presence and power of God's Spirit at work in the lives of believers. The anointing is the empowerment of the Holy Spirit upon a person for a specific purpose or task. Throughout the Bible the anointing is often associated with oil and is used as a symbol of the Holy Spirit's presence and work.

In the Old Testament the anointing of the Holy Spirit was often reserved for kings, prophets, and priests. They were anointed with oil as a symbol of their consecration and empowerment for their specific roles. For example, King David was anointed by Samuel to become the king of Israel, and he later wrote about the anointing in Psalm 23:5, saying, "You anoint my head with oil; my cup overflows."

In the New Testament the anointing of the Holy Spirit takes on a more significant role, as it is available to all believers. Jesus promised His disciples that they would receive the Holy Spirit after His ascension into heaven, and this promise was fulfilled on the day of Pentecost when the Holy Spirit came upon the disciples with power.

In Acts 1:8 Jesus told His disciples, "But you will receive power when the Holy Spirit comes on you; and you will be my witnesses in Jerusalem, and in all Judea and Samaria, and to the ends of the earth." This anointing empowered the disciples to proclaim the gospel and perform miracles in the name of Jesus, fulfilling their calling to be His witnesses.

The anointing of the Holy Spirit is not just for the disciples of Jesus but for all believers. First John 2:20 says, "But you have an anointing from the Holy One, and all of you know the truth." This anointing is the Holy Spirit's presence within us, guiding us in truth and empowering us to live as followers of Jesus.

The anointing of the Holy Spirit is not just a one-time event but an ongoing experience for believers. As we continue to seek and follow Jesus, we can experience the anointing of the Holy Spirit in new and powerful ways. The Holy Spirit helps us to pray, understand the Bible, and live out our faith in practical ways.

The anointing of the Holy Spirit is a significant concept in the Bible. It is the empowerment of the Holy Spirit upon a person for a specific purpose or task. The anointing is available to all believers and is an ongoing experience as we seek and follow Jesus. May we seek the anointing of the Holy Spirit in our lives and be empowered to live as followers of Jesus, proclaiming the gospel and performing works of faith in His name.

LITERAL ANOINTING

As Christians, we believe that we are saved by grace through faith in Jesus Christ and nothing can separate us from the love of God. However, the journey of the Christian life is not without its challenges. The Bible tells us that in the last days there will be an increase in wickedness, and many will fall away from the faith. In order to endure until the end, Christians must have the literal anointing of God.

The concept of anointing is found throughout the Bible. In the Old Testament, kings, priests, and prophets were anointed with oil as a symbol of God's empowerment for their ministry. In the New Testament, we see that Jesus Himself was anointed with the Holy Spirit at His baptism (Luke 3:21–22), and He promised His followers that they too would receive the Holy Spirit (John 14:16–17).

The Holy Spirit is the literal anointing of God. He is the third person of the Trinity, and He empowers us to live the Christian life. Without the Holy Spirit, we would be powerless to resist temptation, to love others as Christ loved us, or to bear witness to the truth of the gospel.

The apostle Paul understood the importance of the Holy Spirit in the life of the believer. In his letter to the Ephesians he writes, "And do not get drunk with wine, for that is debauchery, but be filled with the Spirit" (Eph. 5:18, ESV). The word "filled" here can also be translated as "controlled." Paul is urging the Ephesians (and us) to allow the Holy Spirit to have complete control over our lives.

The literal anointing of God is essential in order for us to endure, because it gives us the strength and power we need to face the challenges of the Christian life. Jesus promised His disciples that the Holy Spirit would be with them always (Matt. 28:20) and guide them into all truth (John 16:13). The Holy Spirit also helps us to pray when we don't know what to pray for (Rom. 8:26–27), and He produces in us the fruit of the Spirit, which includes love, joy, peace, patience, kindness, goodness, faithfulness, gentleness, and self-control (Gal. 5:22–23).

Without the literal anointing of God we are like ships without sails, drifting aimlessly on the sea of life. We may be saved, but we will not have the power we need to live the Christian life to the fullest. We will be more susceptible to temptation, more easily discouraged, and more likely to fall away from the faith.

In conclusion, Christians must have the literal anointing of God in order to endure until the end. The Holy Spirit is the source of our strength and power, and He empowers us to live the Christian life in a way that honors God and bears witness to the truth of the gospel. As we seek to live for Christ, let us pray that we would be filled with the Holy Spirit, and that He would guide us every step of the way.

THE ANOINTING TODAY

The anointing of the Holy Spirit is a powerful force that has been available to Christians since the day of Pentecost, when the Holy Spirit was poured out on the disciples in Jerusalem. The anointing is a special blessing that enables Christians to walk in greater power and authority and to be used by God in ways that are beyond human ability.

Walking in the anointing of the Holy Spirit is a journey that requires a deep commitment to God, a hunger for His presence, and willingness to submit to His will. It involves developing a close relationship with the Holy Spirit through prayer, worship, and studying the Word of God. It also involves willingness to step out in faith and trust the leading of the Holy Spirit, even when this may be uncomfortable or challenging.

One of the primary manifestations of the anointing of the Holy Spirit is the gift of tongues, which is the ability to speak in a language that is unknown to the speaker. This gift is given to believers as a sign of the presence and power of the Holy Spirit and is often accompanied by other gifts such as prophecy, healing, and discernment.

Walking in the anointing of the Holy Spirit also involves being filled with love, joy, peace, patience, kindness, goodness, faithfulness, gentleness, and self-control, which are known as the fruit of the Spirit. These qualities are evidence of the presence of the Holy Spirit in the life of a believer, and they enable Christians to love and serve others in a way that reflects the heart of God.

In addition, walking in the anointing of the Holy Spirit requires a person to be open to the supernatural and to the miraculous power of God. This may involve praying for the sick, casting out demons, or speaking prophetically to others. It may also involve stepping out in faith to do things that are beyond human ability, such as starting a ministry or sharing the gospel with a difficult person. Ultimately, walking in the anointing of the Holy Spirit is about surrendering our lives to God and allowing Him to use us as vessels of His grace and power.

In conclusion, to walk in the anointing of the Holy Spirit we must develop a close relationship with Him, hunger for His presence, be willing to surrender our lives to His will, be filled with the fruit of the Spirit, and be open to the supernatural power of God. May we all strive to walk in Holy Spirit anointing and allow God to use us to bring His love and power to a hurting and broken world.

GUARD THE ANOINTING

I advise all believers to guard the anointing. The anointing can leave us if we are involved in repetitive, unrepentant sin and the Lord decides to remove His blessing and favor from us as a result. Think of the scripture that says, "I know Jesus, and I know Paul, but who are you?" (Acts 19:15, MEV). I never want to be a "Who are you"!

The demons know who walks in the authority and anointing of the Holy Spirit. Someone who is walking righteously, who has a daily relationship with God and is able to go out, cast out, and drive out (*ekballō* in the Greek) has the anointing on them. However, in order to declare and decree, we must also be obedient and enter into the courts of heaven.

The Bible tells us we have the authority to trample on scorpions and devils (Luke 10:19), and "whatever [we] bind on earth will be bound in heaven, and whatever [we] loose on earth will be loosed in heaven" (Matt. 16:19). This authority is based on the anointing of the Holy Spirit. But in order to walk in that anointing, one must be consecrated and submitted to the will of God over his or her life. God will use you in a mighty way if you are willing to lay down your fleshly ambitions and dreams in order to walk out the calling of God on your life.

"As for you, the anointing you received from him remains in you" (1 John 2:27; see also 2 Timothy 1:14).

THE ANOINTING TO SHARE THE GOOD NEWS WITH THE LOST

When I first started in ministry about twenty-three years ago, I was a street preacher. I used to bring my keyboard out and play worship music right on Hollywood Boulevard surrounded by drunk club-goers, homeless people, and druggies. Thank God there wasn't social media back then, as I probably would have been maligned for doing that. But you know what, people got saved, and God met us out there! People would weep and receive prayer and deliverance right there at 2:15 a.m. after the clubs had closed on the street. We need more of this today. We have to bring evangelism back. I know many of you are involved in evangelism, but we need more of it.

I was once one of those lost people in Hollywood, and it was because of obedient people who came out to meet me where I was that I started seeking God. I remember there was a man who would carry a cross right there on Hollywood Boulevard. It was a powerful illustration to those who observed him walking around. Many years ago, when I was a club-goer and used to party in the world, I would walk out of the club and see that man there. Even in my drunken state I was convicted when I saw him, and it planted a seed that would later grow. That man had an anointing to go out and fish for the lost. I was touched by his ministry, and what he did bore fruit. Often we don't realize how much our obedience is touching the lives of others. This is why when the Lord tells us to do something, we should do it.

Jesus hung out with the worst of the worst. People are hungry right now. The harvest is plentiful. There will be times when the wheat and the tares are together. That's just the way it is. However, we are in a season of exposure, and you'd better believe that if someone is up to something nefarious, it will eventually come out.

The Bible says what has been done in darkness will be brought to the light. (See Luke 12:2–3 and 8:17.) I can't spend my time worrying about what this one or that one is up to; however, if someone asks me specifically about a situation, I usually will share what God has shown me about it if I feel prompted to do so.

A TIME FOR CORRECTION

There comes a time when a rebuke issued by an elder in the body of Christ is necessary. Correction is good and should be done in love. We should not allow a spirit of offense or thin skin to stop us from receiving godly wisdom and correction. We should always take it to the Lord and ask the Holy Spirit how we can do better.

Being teachable is a big deal. Each of us must be willing to humbly receive correction and instruction from an elder. The Bible tells us, "Humble yourselves before the Lord, and he will lift you up" (Jas. 4:10). I also talk about eating "humble pie," which means sometimes we listen to what someone says even if we disagree with it to help find common ground and come to a place of healing and reconciliation.

We have an open-door policy here at the ministry. Even if someone has come against us or been critical in the past, we are open to forgiving them and blessing them should they be willing to repent and move forward as brethren. When we are willing to forgive and repent, it pleases God and brings tremendous healing. Often, forgiving isn't even for the benefit of the other person but for us, so we can move on and move forward in victory. However, just because we are called to love people, it doesn't mean we need to be a doormat or their best friend. We can love someone and still guard ourselves. Just because we must love doesn't mean we need to hang out with everyone.

Do not confuse being nice with being a Christian. Because Christians are meant to walk in love and exude the fruit of the Spirit, many people think we should be nice all the time. But remember, Jesus Himself overturned the tables and sometimes acted in righteous anger. I am a firm believer that Christians can be bold, strong, and courageous and still be loving. Being nice isn't always Christlike. We must stand our ground and not be weak or compromise our beliefs to appease others. Part of walking in the anointing is being bold and holding the line. This is the type of Christians we need to be, especially now.

My job is to be as Christlike as I can. Am I perfect? No, far from it. But I have been instructed to go out and share the good news of Jesus Christ and the gospel message to fulfill the Great Commission. It's not my job to have an issue with just about everything and everyone out there. I am called to represent the kingdom of God— truth and righteousness—and to set the captive free by the power of the Holy Spirit with mercy, grace, love, and *biblical truth*! I have been distracted a few times over the years, but when I am, I ask the Holy Spirit to redirect my thoughts and get me back on my mission.

SOULS ARE THE MISSION

If you make souls your mission, God's hand and favor will be on your life. He will anoint you, and the anointing will take you places you never believed you would go. He will open doors and set forth divine appointments on your behalf. The anointing has opened up doors in my life and fostered friendships that only God could have orchestrated. It still blows my mind sometimes. God is so good.

If you make souls your mission, you will not lack. God owns the cattle on a thousand hills and never lacks resources or answers. (See Psalm 50:10.) He has an unlimited supply. You cannot out-give God. When you become a giver and a tither, you will reap a great harvest and receive back, "pressed down, shaken together and running over" (Luke 6:38). When we align our lives with God's purposes, we will see great favor; this is a sure thing. I teach these concepts often because when applied, they always produce the same result and set you up for success.

If you haven't yet received the anointing of the Holy Spirit, receive it today. It's not complicated. Surrender yourself and your life to the living God. Get alone with Him and cry out to Him. Tell God that you want more of Him and that you are ready to fully surrender all of your flesh to receive all He has to give you. God always responds when we pray this way with a sincere heart. He stands at the door of your heart knocking; all you have to do is let Him in. God is looking for willing vessels that He can use. When we allow Him to use us, He will.

SPIRITUAL WARFARE

When someone goes deeper in their walk with Christ or in the ministry, they often notice an uptick in what is known as spiritual warfare. This is because the enemy is mad that there is a deeper level of ministry taking place that in turn will pull people out of darkness and into the light and life of Jesus Christ. The main battle in the world is for the soul of each and every person. Ultimately, that is what it's all about—where each person will spend eternity.

To understand spiritual warfare, we must begin by acknowledging that we are at war. Each of us is engaged in a spiritual battle of light versus darkness.

> For our struggle is not against flesh and blood, but against the rulers, against the authorities, against the powers of this dark world and against the spiritual forces of evil in the heavenly realms.
> —EPHESIANS 6:12

Spiritual warfare is a term that has become popular in Christian circles in recent years. But what does it really mean? From a biblical perspective spiritual warfare refers to the battle that takes place in the spiritual realm between good and evil. This battle is not physical but is fought in the unseen realm, where the forces of darkness seek to destroy the work of God in the lives of His people.

The concept of spiritual warfare is not new, and it is referenced throughout the Bible. As we read in Ephesians 6:12 above, the apostle Paul wrote that the battle we face is not against human beings but against the spiritual forces of evil that seek to oppose God's work in our lives.

The Bible also tells us that our enemy is not flesh and blood but rather Satan and his demons. First Peter 5:8 says, "Be alert and of sober mind. Your enemy the devil prowls around like a roaring lion looking for someone to devour." Satan is a real being who seeks to deceive and destroy God's people, and we must be aware of his tactics if we are to stand firm in our faith.

So, what does spiritual warfare look like in our daily lives? It can take many forms, including temptation, doubt, fear, and discouragement. These are all tactics the enemy uses to try to lead us off course from the path that God has set before us. However, we have been given spiritual weapons to fight this battle. Ephesians 6:13–18 describes the armor of God, which includes the belt of truth, the breastplate of righteousness, the shoes of peace, the shield of faith, the helmet of salvation, and the sword of the Spirit. These weapons are not physical, but they are powerful in the spiritual realm.

Prayer is also a crucial aspect of spiritual warfare. In

Matthew 26:41 Jesus told His disciples, "Watch and pray so that you will not fall into temptation. The spirit is willing, but the flesh is weak." Prayer is our way of communicating with God and asking for His help and protection in the battle we face. We can also pray for our fellow believers, asking God to protect them from the attacks of the enemy.

Finally, we must remember that the victory has already been won. Colossians 2:15 says, "And having disarmed the powers and authorities, he made a public spectacle of them, triumphing over them by the cross." Jesus has already defeated Satan and his demons on the cross, and we have the assurance of victory in Him. We can be confident that no matter what we face in the spiritual realm, we are ultimately on the winning side.

The bottom line is that spiritual warfare is a real battle that we face as Christians, but we have been given the weapons and the assurance of victory through Jesus Christ. We must be aware of the enemy's tactics and be diligent in our prayers and the use of the spiritual weapons that God has given us. Ultimately, we can trust in God's power to protect us and guide us through the battle, knowing the victory has already been won through Christ.

I would advise everyone reading this to get to know and understand the concept of spiritual warfare. Many Christians today ignore this, which is why they are not walking in the fullness of what God has for their lives.

For us to truly come out from among them, we must understand that we are in a battle and use the weapons that God has given us to achieve complete victory in and through Him.

As believers in Christ, we are not exempt from facing battles in our lives. In fact, we are constantly engaged in spiritual warfare, which can be overwhelming at times. There are several battles Christians face that can challenge our faith, but we can take comfort in knowing that we are not alone and God is with us to help us overcome.

One battle that believers in Christ will face is the battle against temptation. We live in a world that is filled with temptation, and it is easy to give in to our fleshly desires. We are bombarded with messages that tell us to indulge in pleasures that are contrary to God's will, and these can be challenging to resist. However, as Christians, we are called to resist the devil and flee from temptation. We can do this by immersing ourselves in the Word of God and staying close to the Lord in prayer.

Another battle that believers face is the battle against doubt. In an increasingly secular world it is easy to doubt our faith and to question whether or not God is real. However, we are called to have faith in God even when we cannot see Him. We can overcome doubt by seeking God in prayer, studying His Word, and surrounding ourselves with other believers who can encourage us in our faith.

A third battle that believers in Christ face today is the

battle against fear. We live in a world that is filled with uncertainty, and it is easy to be afraid of what the future may hold. However, as Christians, we can have peace in the midst of chaos, knowing that God is in control. We can overcome fear by trusting in God's promises, seeking His presence, and focusing on His goodness.

A fourth battle that believers in Christ will face is the battle against complacency. It is easy to become complacent in our faith and go through the motions without truly seeking God's will. However, we are called to be a light in the darkness, and we cannot do that if we are not actively pursuing God. We can overcome complacency by staying connected to God through prayer and by seeking His direction in our lives.

In conclusion, as believers in Christ, we are called to fight the good fight of faith. We may face battles in our lives, but we can take comfort in knowing that God is with us and that He will help us overcome. We can resist temptation, overcome doubt, find peace in the midst of fear, and stay active in our faith by seeking God and trusting in His promises. Let us stand firm in our faith and be a light in the darkness to those around us.

LIFE AND DEATH ARE IN THE TONGUE

As Christians we believe that the power of life and death is in the tongue. Proverbs 18:21 tells us, "The tongue has the power of life and death, and those who love it will eat its fruit." Our words have the ability to bring life or death into our lives and the lives of those around us.

The words we speak have the power to build up or tear down, to encourage or discourage, to give hope or bring despair. Our tongues can be used to spread love, joy, peace, kindness, and the other fruit of the Holy Spirit, or they can be used to spread hate, anger, bitterness, and other works of the flesh.

In the Book of James we are warned about the dangers of the tongue: "The tongue is a small part of the body, but it makes great boasts. Consider what a great forest is set on fire by a small spark. The tongue also is a fire, a world of evil among the parts of the body. It corrupts the whole body, sets the whole course of one's life on fire, and is itself set on fire by hell" (Jas. 3:5–6).

We must be careful with the words we speak because once they are spoken, they cannot be taken back. We must think before we speak and ask ourselves if our words will bring life or death into our situation.

As Christians we are called to use our tongues to build up, not tear down. We are called to speak the truth in love, to encourage one another, to comfort those who are hurting, and to pray for one another. We are called to be light in the darkness and to use our words to bring hope to those who are lost.

However, we must be aware that our words also have the power to bring death. We must guard against using our tongues to spread gossip, to speak words of condemnation, to tear others down, or to speak words of unbelief. We must be careful not to speak curses over our lives or the lives of others but to speak blessings instead.

In Matthew 12:36–37 Jesus warns us that we will be judged for every careless word we speak: "But I tell you that everyone will have to give account on the day of judgment for every empty word they have spoken. For by your words you will be acquitted, and by your words you will be condemned."

Therefore, let us use our tongues to speak life and not death, to build up and not tear down, to bring hope and not despair. Let us speak words of love, joy, peace, patience, kindness, goodness, faithfulness, gentleness, and self-control. Let us use our tongues to glorify God and to bless others. Make sure you are speaking words of life over your situation. This is very important.

In order to come out from among them, we need to have faith that God will indeed order our steps and guide our path. Guard the anointing over your life, and live in a way that pleases the Lord. Again, this will set you up for success. To truly come out from among them, we must walk in the unction and anointing of the Holy Spirit!

CHAPTER 10

THE END-TIME HARVEST

T HE GREAT COMMISSION is a biblical term that refers to the instructions that Jesus Christ gave to His disciples before He ascended into heaven. It is found in the Gospel of Matthew, chapter 28, verses 18–20 (ESV), and it reads: "And Jesus came and said to them, 'All authority in heaven and on earth has been given to me. Go therefore and make disciples of all nations, baptizing them in the name of the Father and of the Son and of the Holy Spirit, teaching them to observe all that I have commanded you. And behold, I am with you always, to the end of the age.'"

This commission is considered one of the most important missions of the Christian faith and is often referred to as the Great Commission because of its magnitude and scope. The Great Commission is an imperative command given to all Christians to spread the good news of Jesus Christ and to make disciples of all nations. In this chapter we will explore what the Great Commission means and its significance in the Christian faith.

The first part of the Great Commission acknowledges Jesus Christ's authority over heaven and earth, indicating that He is the One sending His disciples on this mission. He was given the authority to save people from sin and reconcile them to God. Jesus is the Savior of the world, and His authority gives weight to the command to make disciples of all nations.

The second part of the Great Commission involves going out to all nations to make disciples. This command is not just for pastors, missionaries, or evangelists, but for all believers. Every Christian is called to be a witness of Jesus Christ and share the good news of salvation with those around them. The Great Commission emphasizes the need to reach all nations, which includes people of all races, languages, and cultures.

The third part of the Great Commission is baptizing new believers in the name of the Father, the Son, and the Holy Spirit. Baptism is a public declaration of one's faith in Jesus Christ and symbolizes the washing away of sin and the beginning of a new life in Christ. It is an essential part of the Christian faith and marks the initiation into the Christian community.

The fourth part of the Great Commission is teaching new believers to observe all that Jesus has commanded. This involves helping new believers understand the teachings of Jesus and how to apply them in their daily lives. Discipleship is a lifelong process that involves studying and learning from the Bible and being guided by the Holy Spirit.

The Great Commission is a significant part of the

Christian faith because it is a call to action. It is a call to share the gospel, make disciples, and help others grow in their faith. It is a call to love and serve others and to fulfill the purpose for which we were created. The Great Commission is not just a command, but it is an invitation to participate in the redemptive work of God and to be a part of His plan to save the world.

In conclusion, the Great Commission is a call to action for all Christians. It is a call to share the good news of Jesus Christ, make disciples of all nations, and baptize new believers, teaching them to observe all that Jesus has commanded. The Great Commission is a reminder that we are called to be witnesses of Jesus Christ, to love and serve others, and to fulfill our purpose in the world. It is a commission that we cannot ignore and must take seriously, knowing that Jesus is with us always, even to the end of the age.

MAKE DISCIPLESHIP GREAT AGAIN

Discipleship is a critical aspect of Christianity. It is the process of growing and maturing in faith and being transformed into the image of Christ. During His time on earth, Jesus made it clear that discipleship is essential when He commanded His followers, "Go and make disciples of all nations" (Matt. 28:19).

Discipleship involves sharing the gospel and helping others to grow in their faith. Unfortunately, in recent years many Christians have neglected this important aspect of their faith. Instead they have focused on individualism, materialism, and worldly pursuits. As a result, the church has failed to fulfill its mandate of making disciples.

It is crucial that Christians start making disciples again. Here are some reasons why.

It is a command from Jesus.

As I mentioned earlier, Jesus commanded His followers to go and make disciples. This command is not optional but rather a critical aspect of being a Christian. As followers of Christ it is our duty to obey His commands, including the command to make disciples.

It is the only way to fulfill the Great Commission.

The Great Commission is a call to make disciples of all nations. If we fail to make disciples, we will not fulfill this critical aspect of the Great Commission. This means that millions of people around the world will be left without the opportunity to hear the gospel and grow in their faith.

It is a sign of spiritual maturity.

Discipleship is important not only for those being discipled but also for those doing the discipling. When we disciple others, we grow in our own faith and become more spiritually mature. We learn to depend on God and become more like Christ.

It is a way to impact the world for Christ.

Making disciples is a powerful way to impact the world for Christ. When we disciple others, we are helping to build up the church, which is the body of Christ. As the church grows, it has a greater impact on the world around us.

It is a way to leave a lasting legacy.

When we invest in the lives of others, we are leaving a lasting legacy. The people we disciple will go on to disciple others, creating a chain reaction that will impact generations to come.

In conclusion, it is essential that Christians start making disciples again. Discipleship is a critical aspect of our faith, and without it we cannot fulfill the Great Commission. As we make disciples, we impact the world for Christ, grow in our own faith, and leave a lasting legacy. Let us therefore commit ourselves to making disciples and fulfilling the call of Christ to go and make disciples of all nations.

WHAT IS THE HARVEST?

The term *harvest* appears frequently in the Bible and holds great significance. The concept of harvest is used to describe not only the physical act of reaping crops but also spiritual and metaphorical ideas such as judgment, blessing, and salvation.

In the Bible the word *harvest* is most commonly

associated with gathering crops, particularly in the Old Testament. In ancient Israel, harvest time was a time of great celebration and thanksgiving to God for providing food and sustenance for the people. The harvest was a crucial event in the agricultural society of ancient Israel, as the success of the harvest determined whether or not the people would have enough food to survive the coming year.

The agricultural metaphor of harvest is also used throughout the Bible to convey spiritual ideas. For instance, in the New Testament the term *harvest* is often used to describe the final judgment of humanity. This is seen in passages such as Matthew 13:39, where Jesus says, "The harvest is the end of the age, and the harvesters are angels." Here the harvest represents the end of the world and the separation of the righteous from the unrighteous.

Similarly, the harvest is also used in the Bible to describe the salvation of souls. In John 4:35–38 Jesus uses the metaphor of a harvest to teach His disciples about the importance of spreading the gospel: "I tell you, open your eyes and look at the fields! They are ripe for harvest. Even now the one who reaps draws a wage and harvests a crop for eternal life, so that the sower and the reaper may be glad together." Here the harvest represents the gathering of people into the kingdom of God.

Moreover, the term *harvest* is also used in the Bible to describe the blessings that God bestows upon His people. In Leviticus 26:3–5 God promises to bless His people with an abundant harvest if they obey His commandments: "If you follow my decrees and are careful to obey my commands, I will send you rain in its season, and the ground will yield its crops and the trees their fruit."

THE LABORERS ARE FEW

The Bible contains divine insights into the human condition and the challenges faced by man throughout history. One theme that emerges in the Bible is the scarcity of laborers to gather the harvest. Isn't it interesting that the job the Bible asks us to do in the Great Commission is the very area in which there is a major labor shortage? What does that tell us about humanity and our rebellion against the ways of God? We can't seem to do even the one thing He has asked of us. Is the church today also guilty of this?

The idea of labor shortage is first mentioned in the New Testament in the Gospel of Matthew. In chapter 9 Jesus sees the crowds of people who are following Him and feels compassion for them because they are like sheep without a shepherd. He then tells His disciples, "The harvest is plentiful, but the laborers are few; therefore pray earnestly to the Lord of the harvest to send out laborers into his harvest" (Matt. 9:37–38, esv).

This metaphor of the harvest and the laborers has been interpreted in many different ways over the centuries, but one common understanding is that it refers to the need for people to do the work of spreading the gospel and caring for the spiritual needs of others. In this interpretation, the "harvest" represents the people who are ready to hear the good news of Jesus, and the "laborers" are the people who are willing and able to share that message with others.

This idea of a scarcity of laborers is echoed in other parts of the Bible as well. In the Book of Isaiah, for example, the prophet writes, "The LORD saw it, and it displeased him that there was no justice. He saw that there was no man, and wondered that there was no one to intercede" (Isa. 59:15–16, ESV). Here the idea of a shortage of people who are willing to do the work of advocating for justice and righteousness is highlighted.

So, what can we learn from this theme of labor shortage in the Bible? One lesson is that the work of serving others and sharing the message of God's love is an important and urgent task that requires the participation of many people. It's also God's heart for us. It is not something that can be left to a few dedicated individuals or professionals. We are all called to be laborers in the spiritual harvest, to use our talents and abilities to help others and share the good news of Jesus Christ.

Another lesson is that the scarcity of laborers is not a new problem. It has been a challenge throughout history, and it continues to be a challenge today. There are many people in our communities who are hungry for spiritual guidance and support, and many who are in need of practical assistance and care. We can each do our part to be laborers in this harvest, to seek out opportunities to serve others and share the message of God's love. We must do better in this area as well. It is pivotal to our very freedoms as a people.

The theme of labor shortage in the Bible is a reminder of the importance of our role as laborers in the spiritual harvest. We are all called to use our talents and abilities to serve others and share the message of God's love. May we each be inspired by this call, and may we work together to meet the needs of those around us.

THE END-TIME HARVEST

The concept of the end-time harvest of souls is a prominent theme in the Bible, particularly in the New Testament. It refers to the final gathering of people who will be saved and enter into eternal life, and those who will be lost and face eternal damnation. The harvest of souls is a profound topic that requires an understanding of biblical teachings and eschatology.

The term *harvest* is used metaphorically in the Bible to refer to the gathering of people at the end of the age, where Jesus Christ will separate the righteous from the unrighteous. This is often referred to as the "Great White Throne Judgment" (Rev. 20:11–15), where all the dead will be raised, and every person will stand before God to give an account of their lives.

The concept of the end-time harvest of souls is closely related to the biblical doctrine of salvation. The Bible teaches that salvation is a free gift from God, and it is obtained by faith in Jesus Christ (Eph. 2:8–9). This means salvation is not earned by good works, but rather it is a result of God's grace.

The end-time harvest of souls is a critical component of eschatology, the study of the end times. According to the Bible, the end times will be marked by several significant events, including the rapture of the church, the rise of the Antichrist, the seven-year tribulation, and the return of Jesus Christ. The end-time harvest of souls will occur at the end of this period.

The Bible describes the end-time harvest of souls in several places. One of the best-known passages is Matthew 13:24–30, where Jesus tells the parable of the wheat and the tares. In this parable a man sows good seed, but an enemy comes and plants weeds among the wheat in his field. The wheat and tares grow together until the harvest, where the wheat is gathered into the barn and the tares are burned.

Jesus later explains the parable to His disciples, saying, "The field is the world, and the good seed stands for the people of the kingdom. The weeds are the people of the evil one, and the enemy who sows them is the devil" (Matt. 13:38–39). The harvest represents the end of the age, and the reapers are the angels who will separate the righteous from the unrighteous.

Another passage that describes the end-time harvest of souls is found in Revelation 14:14–20, where John sees a vision of a white cloud with someone sitting on it who is described as having a golden crown and a sharp sickle. An angel comes out of the temple and tells the one sitting on the cloud to harvest the earth, for it is ripe for the picking. The one sitting on the cloud swings his sickle, and the earth is harvested.

The symbolism in this passage is rich and significant. The one sitting on the cloud represents Jesus Christ, who is the ultimate judge of the world. The sharp sickle represents the judgment of God, and the harvest represents the end-time gathering of people. The grapes that are harvested represent the unrighteous, who will be thrown into the winepress of the wrath of God and face eternal punishment.

The end-time harvest of souls is a sobering reminder that we are living in the last days and time is short. The Bible teaches that we should be ready for the return of Jesus Christ, for we do not know the day or the hour when He will come (Matt. 24:36). We should be diligent in our walk with God and live our lives in a way that is pleasing to Him.

"Thrust in thy sickle, and reap: for the time is come for thee to reap; for the harvest of the earth is ripe" (Rev. 14:15, KJV).

THE TIME IS NOW

One of the fundamental beliefs of Christianity is that Jesus Christ will return to earth someday. While the exact timing of this event is unknown, the Bible makes it clear that it will happen. As such, it's essential that we get as many people saved as possible before this event occurs. Here is why this is important.

First, as Christians we believe that salvation is necessary to gain entrance to heaven. John 3:16 says, "For God so loved the world that he gave his one and only Son, that whoever believes in him shall not perish but have eternal life." This means the only way to enter heaven is through faith in Jesus Christ. Therefore, it is crucial that we share the gospel with as many people as possible so that they too may receive salvation.

Second, we believe that salvation is not just about gaining entry to heaven; it is also about having a relationship with God. When someone receives salvation, they become a child of God, and their relationship with Him is restored. This relationship is essential for spiritual growth and the fulfillment of our purpose on earth. Therefore, sharing the gospel is not just about getting people into heaven but also about bringing them into a meaningful relationship with God.

Third, we believe that salvation is the only way to be saved from eternal separation from God. Revelation 20:15 says, "Anyone whose name was not found written in the book of life was thrown into the lake of fire." Those who do not receive salvation will be separated from God for eternity. As Christians we do not want anyone to experience this fate, which is why it's important that we share the gospel and give people the opportunity to accept Jesus Christ as their Lord and Savior.

Fourth, we believe that sharing the gospel is a commandment from Jesus. In Mark 16:15 Jesus said, "Go into all the world and preach the gospel to all creation." It is not just a good idea to share the gospel but a commandment from our Lord and Savior. As Christians we must obey this commandment and do our best to share the gospel with as many people as possible.

Finally, we believe that the return of Jesus Christ is imminent. In Matthew 24:44 Jesus said, "So you also must be ready, because the Son of Man will come at an hour when you do not expect him." We do not know when Jesus will return, and we must be ready at all times. The best way to be ready is to share the gospel with as many people as possible so that they too may be prepared for His return.

As Christians we have a responsibility to share the gospel with as many people as possible, and we should do so with urgency and love. Our Messiah Jesus will be coming back soon. In order to come out from among them, we need to get people saved; then they too can wake up and be set apart for such a time as this!

CHAPTER 11

THE UNDERGROUND RAILROAD FOR THE REMNANT

THE UNDERGROUND RAILROAD was a secret network of people, both black and white, who helped enslaved people escape from slavery in the United States. It operated from the late eighteenth century to the time of the Civil War and was so named because of its use of railway terminology: "stations" were safe houses, "conductors" were guides, and "passengers" were the enslaved people being helped to escape.

The Underground Railroad was not an actual railroad but a complex system of safe houses and routes that were used to transport slaves from the South to the North, where they could be free. The network of people who helped run the Underground Railroad included abolitionists, former slaves, and sympathetic individuals who believed in the cause of freedom.

The Underground Railroad was a dangerous and illegal operation, and those who participated risked their lives and freedom. The people who ran the safe houses and provided food, clothing, and shelter to escaped slaves were known as "station masters." They were often Quakers or members of other religious groups who opposed slavery and believed in equal rights for all people.

The escape routes of the Underground Railroad were secret and varied, with different routes and methods used in different regions. Some slaves escaped by foot, while others traveled by wagon, boat, or even train. The conductors, many of whom were former slaves themselves, would guide the escaping slaves along the route, sometimes using a code language to communicate with other conductors and station masters along the way.

The Underground Railroad played an important role in the abolition of slavery in the United States. It helped thousands of enslaved people escape to freedom, and it helped raise awareness of the injustices of slavery. The courage and dedication of those involved in the Underground Railroad paved the way for the eventual end of slavery in the United States.

THE UNDERGROUND CHURCH IN CHINA TODAY

The underground church in China is a modern underground railroad type of system that is also known as the house church. It is a vibrant and growing movement of believers who have chosen to worship outside the official government-sanctioned church at high risk. This movement has been able to survive and thrive despite intense government persecution, and this is a testament to the strength and resilience of the Chinese Christian community.

From a Christian perspective, the underground church in China represents a remarkable expression of faith and devotion in the face of tremendous adversity. These believers are willing to risk imprisonment, torture, and even death to remain faithful to their beliefs and share the gospel with others. They understand that their faith is not something to be kept hidden or confined to a particular building or institution, but rather something to be lived out in every aspect of their lives.

One of the key reasons the underground church has been able to survive and thrive in China is because of its decentralized and flexible structure. Unlike the official government-sanctioned church, which is tightly controlled and monitored by the state, the house church is made up of small groups of believers who meet in homes, apartments, or other private spaces discreetly. This allows them to avoid detection by the authorities and to worship freely without interference.

Another factor that has contributed to the success of the underground church is its strong sense of community and fellowship. Believers in the house church often come from marginalized and persecuted backgrounds, and they find community and support in their shared Christian faith. They care for one another, share their struggles and joys, and encourage one another to remain steadfast in their faith, no matter what challenges they may face.

The underground church in China is also thriving because of its commitment to evangelism and discipleship. Despite the risks involved, believers are passionate about sharing the gospel with others and seeing lives transformed by the power of God. They recognize that their faith is not just a private matter but something that must be shared with the world. They make the mission about souls and are fulfilling the Great Commission.

Perhaps most importantly, the underground church in China is thriving because of its unwavering commitment to Jesus Christ. These believers are not motivated by political or social agendas but by a deep and abiding love for Jesus. They are willing to suffer and even die for their faith because they believe it is the truth and that it offers hope and salvation to all who believe, which is true.

The underground church in China is a remarkable expression of faith and resilience in the face of persecution. It is a testament to the power of the gospel and the transformative work of the Holy Spirit in the lives of believers. As we pray for our brothers and sisters in China, let us also be inspired by their example of faith and commitment to Christ.

WHO WAS DIETRICH BONHOEFFER?

Dietrich Bonhoeffer was a German theologian and pastor who lived during the turbulent years leading up to World War II. Despite being born into a privileged and conservative family, Bonhoeffer became a vocal critic of the Nazi regime and a leading figure in the resistance movement. His bravery, moral courage, and unwavering commitment to justice have made him a hero to many people around the world.

Bonhoeffer was born in Breslau, Germany (now Wrocław, Poland), in 1906. From a young age, he showed an exceptional talent for theology and philosophy. After completing his studies in Germany, he went to the United States to further his education, where he became involved in the ecumenical movement and was introduced to influential figures such as Reinhold Niebuhr.[1]

In 1931 Bonhoeffer returned to Germany and began teaching at the University of Berlin. He quickly became a prominent voice in the Confessing Church, a movement of Protestant Christians who opposed the Nazi regime and refused to align themselves with the state-controlled German Evangelical church. Bonhoeffer's opposition to the Nazis was rooted in his Christian faith, which taught him to stand up for the oppressed and defend the innocent.

As the Nazis tightened their grip on Germany, Bonhoeffer became increasingly involved in the resistance movement. He helped establish an underground seminary for Confessing Church pastors and played a key role in the Abwehr, the German military intelligence agency, where he used his contacts to aid the resistance. Bonhoeffer also played a role in several failed attempts to assassinate Adolf Hitler.[2]

In 1943 Bonhoeffer was arrested by the Gestapo and charged with treason. He spent the next two years in prison, where he continued to write and reflect on his faith. One of his most famous works, *Letters and Papers from Prison*, was written during this time. In it he explored the relationship between religion and politics and argued that true Christianity required active resistance to tyranny and oppression.

Despite the danger to his own life Bonhoeffer never wavered in his commitment to justice and the defense of the oppressed. He refused to compromise his beliefs or collaborate with the Nazi regime, even when offered the opportunity to do so in exchange for his freedom. On April 9, 1945, just a few weeks before the end of the war, he was executed by hanging at Flossenbürg concentration camp.

Today, Bonhoeffer is remembered as a hero and a martyr for his unwavering commitment to justice and his refusal to remain silent in the face of evil. His legacy continues to inspire people around the world to stand up for what is right and to fight for justice, even in the face of overwhelming opposition.

WHAT CAN WE LEARN FROM THIS?

Bonhoeffer's story has many important lessons relevant for Christians today. Here are some key lessons that we can learn from his life:

The importance of living out our faith in the real world

One of the most striking things about Bonhoeffer's life is that he didn't just talk about his faith; he lived it out in the real world. He was deeply committed to biblical truth and worked tirelessly to help those who were marginalized and oppressed. He also spoke out against the evils of the Nazi regime and was willing to risk his own life to try to bring an end to the atrocities that were being committed.

Christians today can follow Bonhoeffer's example by getting involved in our communities and working to make a difference in the world. We can't just sit back and wait for others to do the work for us. We need to be actively engaged in the world, using our gifts and talents to make a positive impact.

The importance of speaking out against tyranny

Bonhoeffer was not afraid to speak out against the injustice that he saw around him. He spoke out against the Nazi regime and its policies of racism, persecution, and genocide. He recognized that silence in the face of evil is not an option for Christians.

Christians today need to follow Bonhoeffer's example by speaking out against evil wherever we see it. We need to be willing to stand up for religious freedom even when it's difficult or unpopular. We can't remain silent in the face of injustice and expect things to get better.

The importance of deepening our faith through prayer and study

Bonhoeffer was a deeply spiritual person who was committed to prayer and study. He recognized that the Christian faith is not just about doing good works but about cultivating a deep relationship with God.

Christians today can learn from Bonhoeffer's example by making prayer and study a priority in our lives. We need to spend time in prayer seeking God's guidance and wisdom. We also need to study the Bible and other Christian writings so that we can deepen our understanding of the faith and grow in our relationship with God.

The importance of community and fellowship

Bonhoeffer recognized the importance of community and fellowship in the Christian life. He believed that we are not meant to live out our faith in isolation but rather in the context of a supportive community.

Christians today can learn from Bonhoeffer's example by seeking out community and fellowship with other believers. We need to be a part of a church or other Christian community where we can worship, learn, and grow together. We also need to be intentional about building relationships with other Christians so that we can support and encourage one another in our faith.

The importance of standing up for what is right, even when it's difficult

Bonhoeffer's involvement in the plot to assassinate Hitler was a controversial and risky decision. He knew that he was putting his own life on the line, but he believed that it was the right thing to do in order to bring an end to the evil that was rising up in his time. We must do the same.

GOD GAVE ME A VISION

The Lord has spoken to me for many years about starting an "underground railroad for the remnant." When I first heard this, I had no idea what God was telling me to do. It took a lot of prayer and really seeking His heart to understand what He was saying.

I believe we are in a unique period of time and that this season will not last too much longer. This is a time of preparation and separation before we go to our destination. God showed me that we will indeed see a massive end-time harvest unlike anything we have ever seen before. But He also showed me that simultaneously the creature comforts of the world will not be as readily available as they have been our whole lives up until now. Things are about to change. Supply chains will be disrupted even more than they were during COVID; I believe that was only a test run for what is coming down the pike in the near future.

At some point in the next ten to twenty years the freedoms that we have now will be greatly diminished. The United States will no longer be the superpower it is today, as the central planners have designed it this way in order to achieve their future plans—this is laid out in their writings and charters.

China has been propped up due to its lack of individual freedom and its ability to control its people in a way that the elites would like to see mainstreamed throughout the world. I consider it a test country for the globalists. Restrictions of religious freedom, mobility, and basic human rights that we enjoy in the West and take for granted are not available to citizens of Communist China.

The social credit system that is already in motion in China is being slowly rolled out in the West by means of banks and corporations. It is a sneak attack, as many don't realize how much of their lives are tracked. Modern quantum computers can easily hold a file on every single citizen on the planet. The data is already being compiled for future use. This is why it seems that our own intel communities are taking aim at American citizens now. During the pandemic, some American pastors were arrested for simply wanting to keep their churches open, a basic constitutional right that would have never been infringed upon only a few decades ago. Yet here we are—an America where the FBI labels parents possible terror threats for simply not wanting their kids to be forced to wear masks.

I believe one of my main callings is to prepare the remnant for what is to come. We need to establish an infrastructure and foster communities throughout the country that can circle the wagons and help each other as things progress. I envision a season where significant amounts of trading and bartering will become necessary. I also believe that some people may need to be housed and even hidden away as persecution rises to levels similar to what we are seeing in China. We need to learn from and study the wins and key takeaways of the house churches and underground churches in China, as this will help us prepare and be ready when this time comes.

It would only take some type of major event on the level of COVID or 9/11 to cause a major economic collapse—which may already be planned—in order to set into place a new form of government structure worldwide. Most people don't want to think of something so dark, but in reality, those who are studying current events can connect the dots and read material on many of the elites' own websites and speeches to determine that this type of thinking isn't as far out as it may appear. While I believe we still have a little more time, now is the time to prepare, as we may not have as long as some people think. I am determined to spend these next few years preparing and equipping those with ears to hear about such things. Some will fare better than others when this time comes.

REMNANT REVIVAL CENTERS

God has also been speaking to me about establishing "Remnant Revival Centers" around the country and the world. These would not be your typical churches but would be open every day of the week and allow the fivefold ministry giftings to take place in synchrony by hosting various events and different functions and gatherings throughout the week. One night may be a night of worship, another night a church service, and another may be a workshop or night of prayer. I've never understood why we don't do something along these lines. The church needs to be much more active and involved. We have to foster an environment where we can truly train up and equip people. We need to tone down the performance and tone up the discipleship!

Each Remnant Revival Center would perform these functions in the community:

- It would be an active house of prayer.

- It would conduct services and Bible studies.

- It would hold key classes equipping and activating the saints.

- It would be a place where people can go and receive prayer for deliverance.

- It would be a place where people can go to get sound biblical counseling.

- It would hold worship sets and powerful worship events.

- It would allow for all fivefold ministry giftings to take place and bring in these ministers from all over the world to speak.

- It would be a hub for resources, meet the key needs of the community, and be a storehouse for times of need, providing food and other essential resources should there be a breakdown in our society in supply chains.

- And so much more!

Think about a place that is designed for the teaching, edification, equipping, and encouraging of the saints! This is so needed, especially right now. This is *not* a denomination…this is the *ekklesia*!

The vision is big, and in our humanity it seems almost impossible—but God! Think about how critical these centers will be as the world around us continues to get more and more challenging. How can we as a church prepare and be set up for success in the days, months, and years ahead? We are called to "occupy until He comes."

This is not the only answer. This is one answer. Other believers will get different visions, of course!

We have to start somewhere. The beta test, or first Remnant Revival Center, will be in Nashville, Tennessee. It will cost around $400,000 to get it off the ground and fully operational. We are praying that the resources for this project come in soon. Please keep us in your prayers as well.

COME OUT FROM AMONG THEM

The phrase "come out from among them" appears in several places in the Bible, including 2 Corinthians 6:17 and Revelation 18:4.

In 2 Corinthians 6:14–18 the apostle Paul is exhorting the Corinthians to not be unequally yoked with unbelievers. Then in verse 17 he quotes Isaiah 52:11, saying, "Therefore, 'Come out from them and be separate, says the Lord. Touch no unclean thing, and I will receive you.'"

In the context of this passage, the "them" Paul is referring to are unbelievers who do not share the faith and values of the Christians. The command to "come out from among them" is a call to separate oneself from their way of life and values and to live a holy and righteous life that is pleasing to God. This does not necessarily mean physical separation from nonbelievers but rather a separation in terms of values, priorities, and actions.

In context, Revelation 18:4 is a warning to believers to separate themselves from the sinful practices and values of Babylon, which is symbolic of the world's corrupt and godless systems. The command to "come out from among them" is a call to renounce participation in these sinful practices and avoid being caught up in the judgment that is to come.

To summarize, the phrase "come out from among them" is a call for believers to separate themselves from the values and practices of the world and to live in a way that is holy and pleasing to God.

What I hope you take away from reading this book is an understanding that we can no longer operate as business as usual. We must live with a sense of urgency. I pray that each of you would inquire of the Holy Spirit and ask the Lord if these things are in fact true.

I also hope you understand that we as Christians can no longer live immersed in the world's evil system. It is imperative that the church and people of God understand the need to know the Word, hide it in our hearts, and apply it—live it out. We must make it our priority to be about the business of the Lord and come out from among the evil and wickedness of this Babylonian system and truly be set apart. We cannot partake in their rituals and their idolatry. We cannot be lovers of God and also lovers of mammon (Matt. 6:24, KJV). What place does light have with darkness? (See 2 Corinthians 6:14.)

The compromise must stop. It's time for us to come back to the heart of worship. We need to look back to the original church, get rid of the traditions of man and religion, and be followers of the Way once again. Jesus is "the way, the truth, and the life" (John 14:6, KJV). We must do what it takes to consecrate ourselves and close any open doors of sin, as the enemy will use whatever doors we leave open. It's time to get serious about our walk and avoid even the appearance of evil. This is how we come out from among them!

CHAPTER 12

FOR SUCH A TIME AS THIS

THE PHRASE "FOR such a time as this" comes from the Book of Esther in the Bible. In it, Esther, a Jewish woman, becomes queen of Persia at a critical time when the Jewish people are facing extermination. Esther's cousin Mordecai urges her to use her position to help save her people, telling her, "Who knows but that you have come to your royal position for such a time as this?" (Est. 4:14).

For believers in Jesus Christ today, this phrase serves as a reminder that God has a purpose for their lives and they may be called to play a significant role in God's plan at a particular time and place. Just as Esther was called to be in a position of influence at a critical moment, believers can trust that God has placed them where they are for a reason and that they can make a difference in the world around them.

This phrase also encourages believers to be bold and courageous in following God's calling, even if it means taking risks and facing challenges. Esther was willing to put her own life on the line to save her people, and believers may be called to make sacrifices and take risks for the sake of God's kingdom.

Esther was a remarkable woman. She was known for her beauty, courage, and wisdom, and her story is an inspiring example of how faith, courage, and determination can make a difference even in the most challenging situations.

The Book of Esther tells the story of a Jewish girl named Hadassah, who is also known as Esther, living in Persia during the reign of King Xerxes. Esther was an orphan raised by her cousin Mordecai, who was also a Jewish exile in Persia. Esther was known for her beauty, and her captivating charm caught the attention of King Xerxes, who chose her as his queen.

The story of Esther takes a dramatic turn when Haman, an adviser to the king, plots to exterminate all the Jews in the Persian Empire. Mordecai, who had refused to bow down to Haman, had infuriated him, and Haman sought revenge by convincing the king to issue a decree to exterminate all the Jews in the empire. Mordecai urged Esther to use her position as queen to save her people.

Esther faced a difficult decision. She knew that approaching the king without being summoned could result in her death, but she also knew that her silence could mean the death of all her people. Esther showed great courage and faith by risking her life to approach the king and reveal Haman's evil plan. The king was outraged, Haman was executed, and the Jews were saved.

Esther's courage and faith are celebrated every year during the Jewish festival of Purim. The festival, which is held on the fourteenth and fifteenth days of the Jewish month of Adar, commemorates the deliverance of the Jews from the hands of their enemies.

The story of Esther is not only a story of courage and faith but also a story of how God uses ordinary people to accomplish His purposes. Esther was an ordinary girl, but God used her in a significant way to save her people. Esther's story reminds us that even in the midst of difficult circumstances, we can trust God to give us the courage and strength we need to overcome our challenges. The Book of Esther is a testimony to the power of faith and the triumph of good over evil.

Esther's story is one of bravery and heroism. She risked her life to save her people from annihilation. Her story has been an inspiration to many for centuries, and the lessons it teaches us about courage, faith, and selflessness are still relevant today.

I believe God is raising up a new generation of Esthers. But what does it mean to be a modern-day Esther? What significance does this hold for us as a society?

First and foremost, modern-day Esthers serve as examples of courage and bravery in the face of spiritual warfare and attacks on biblical Christianity. Just as Esther stood up to King Xerxes and risked her life to save her people, modern-day Esthers stand up to social pressures, persecution, and the bias systems designed to oppress and harm the people of God. These women of God are bold and unafraid. We often refer to them as "mama bears."

By embodying the spirit of Esther, modern-day Esthers remind us of the importance of standing up for what is right, even in the face of great risk and spiritual attacks. They inspire us to take action, speak out, and boldly stand for our faith in God.

Moreover, modern-day Esthers serve as symbols of hope and possibility. They demonstrate that change is possible, that one person can make a difference. Their stories inspire us to believe in our own power to effect change when we are empowered by God to be about His business.

By lifting up the stories and achievements of modern-day Esthers, we can counter the cancel culture that so often tries to dominate our public discourse. Women of God have an important role to play in taking back the territory and coming out from among them!

Just as Esther relied on the support of her fellow Jews, modern-day Esthers draw strength from the communities that surround them. They work in partnership with others to effect change, recognizing that true transformation requires collective action in faith. I am encouraged to see women of God rising up throughout the body of Christ. The significance of having modern-day Esthers cannot be overstated. These courageous individuals serve as examples, symbols, and inspirations for us all. They remind us of the power of one person to make a difference, the possibility of change, and the importance of having community and solidarity with others of like mind.

We, like Esther, have important choices to make. God

is looking for people today who will be brave and take a stand much like Esther did. We have significant choices that are put before us each and every day. We too must be a people of faith and action. Esther took a great risk and relied on her faith in God to get her through.

Most of us know the story of David and Goliath. David faced the giant Goliath, who clearly had more physical strength and better armor, yet David had the favor of God and walked out his calling. This action took him from the lowliest place to eventually ruling the entire nation of Israel.

There are modern-day Esthers and Davids reading this right now who are being inspired by the Holy Spirit to accomplish something big in this critical hour. While there are many challenges and threats before us and it is easy to feel overwhelmed, God isn't out of moves, nor has He forsaken us. If we make souls our mission, God will bless us and put His favor on us.

It is imperative that the church align with God's plan and His will in this hour. We must return to the basics and return to our first love, Jesus Christ. We must remember that God is not done. As long as we are here, there is work to be done, and we can and will experience great miracles, signs, and wonders.

It's time for the glorious church to rise up and come out from among them. As we do, we will see a massive end-time harvest and experience the glory and presence of the most high God. Don't let another day of apathy or complacency happen. It's go time. You were made for a time such as this.

A SEASON OF RECALIBRATION

The system is corrupt; I know it, you know it, and I think more people than are willing to admit it know it as well. We can become extremely discouraged if we sit and wallow in this reality. So many egregious things are happening in our nation and world. If we allow our emotions and flesh to dictate where we exist in the natural, it can make us feel helpless and small. Yet we serve a supernatural God! He never runs out of solutions! We will always stand for truth and righteousness, period. We are not citizens of this world; we are in it but not of it!

As I was reading the Bible yesterday, I was reminded of this scripture:

> Finally, brethren, whatsoever things are true, what-
> soever things are honest, whatsoever things are
> just, whatsoever things are pure, whatsoever things
> are lovely, whatsoever things are of good report;
> if there be any virtue, and if there be any praise,
> think on these things.
> —PHILIPPIANS 4:8, KJV

The truth is, we are not defeated. If we have Jesus in our hearts and are living for Him, we can live an abundant life! The term *abundant life* is mentioned in the

Bible in John 10:10, where Jesus says, "The thief comes only to steal and kill and destroy; I have come that they may have life, and have it to the full." This verse is often interpreted to mean that Jesus came to offer a life that is abundant and full of meaning, purpose, and joy.

The abundant life referred to in the Bible is not necessarily a life of material abundance, but a life that is rich in spiritual and emotional well-being. It is a life in which one is free from the burden of sin and guilt and is able to experience the love, peace, and joy that come from a relationship with God.

The abundant life is characterized by a deep sense of fulfillment, contentment, and purpose as well as an awareness of the presence of God in one's life. It is a life that is marked by a willingness to serve others, to love unconditionally, and to live in accordance with God's will.

Do we believe this? Do we walk in it?

As believers we have the answer for this dying world. His name is Jesus Christ. He is the author and finisher of our story. He has *not* forsaken us! It's time for us to press in and go deeper than ever before. So many are in serious need right now. So many are broken and hurting. So many are confused and depressed. So many are searching for answers to life's biggest challenges and questions.

We must respond to these people in need. There is a tremendous harvest out there waiting to be tended to! Our mission must be souls. We must respond and fulfill the Great Commission!

Here is where the recalibration is happening in our ministry. God has given us a mandate to make it about *souls*. It's time to focus on what is *kingdom*. The church has the authority to pull down the strongholds in this nation! The church must be activated, equipped, and sent out. We must occupy until He comes.

I am not disappointed, discouraged, or depressed. We are literally just getting started! This is the time we were made to be alive! Hallelujah!

OUR MANDATE: BUILD AN ALTERNATIVE ECOSYSTEM

As I have mentioned throughout the book, there is a significant need for the people of God to come out from among the Babylonian system. This will require us to develop our own ecosystems. We can no longer have our rights dictated to us by woke corporations, biased social media platforms, activist schools, and many other groups who wish to silence, censor, restrict, and take away the rights and freedoms of Christians. As persecution rises, we need to have the infrastructure and systems in place to resist and thwart the plans of the enemy.

Many of you have been given visions and dreams of ways to do these things. Don't wait until it's too late to walk out the calling of God and the vision He has given you. We must foster an environment where we can have our own...everything! From movie and TV studios to health care, banking, schools, stores, cell phone companies—you name it! Christians need to be entrepreneurial visionaries in this hour. We must walk forward in a way that sets us up for success. We can also use the court systems and other means to take a stand for religious liberty and freedom and push back. Alternative ecosystems provide a safe haven for us to operate outside the cancel culture's dictates and confines.

Christians must preserve our rights and freedoms by using the necessary means to take a stand and develop clear alternatives to the broken and compromised systems in which the world wants us to participate. By developing these alternative systems, we will subsequently strengthen our position and complicate the plans to target us and shut us down.

It's time for us to get comfortable with being uncomfortable and operate in the big faith needed to accomplish the mission. This generation will be the ones who restore the foundations and return to biblical morality and the fundamentals of our faith. As we do this, we will see a massive end-time harvest of souls and a great move of the Holy Spirit. I can sense that we are on the cusp of something big and that God is about to move in a mighty and powerful way. The key is that we as the people of God get serious about our faith, go deeper than ever before, and truly come out from among them, in Jesus' name!

ENDNOTES

CHAPTER 1

1. Christopher Cone, "Are Christians Supposed to Judge Others?" Sharper Iron, September 22, 2015, https://sharperiron.org/article/are-christians-supposed-to-judge-others.

CHAPTER 2

1. "What Was the Babylonian Captivity/Exile?," Got Questions, accessed March 7, 2023, https://www.gotquestions.org/Babylonian-captivity-exile.html.
2. "What Was the Babylonian Captivity/Exile?," Got Questions.
3. Ashley Lutz, "These 6 Corporations Control 90% of the Media in America," Business Insider, June 14, 2012, https://www.businessinsider.com/these-6-corporations-control-90-of-the-media-in-america-2012-6.
4. "Modeling the Future of Religion in America," Pew Research Center, September 13, 2022, https://www.pewresearch.org/religion/2022/09/13/modeling-the-future-of-religion-in-america/.

CHAPTER 3

1. Jessica A. Knoblauch, "Some Food Additives Mimic Human Hormones," *Scientific American*, March 27, 2009, https://www.scientificamerican.com/article/food-additives-mimic-hormones/.
2. Will Sullivan, "Human Sperm Counts Declining Worldwide, Study Finds," *Smithsonian Magazine*, November 22, 2022, https://www.smithsonianmag.com/smart-news/human-sperm-counts-declining-worldwide-study-finds-180981138/#:~:text=In%20the%20last%20

50%20years,published%20between%201973%20and%20
2018.

3. Rosie Gray, "An NSC Staffer Is Forced Out Over a
Controversial Memo," *The Atlantic*, August 2, 2017, https://
www.theatlantic.com/politics/archive/2017/08/a-national-
security-council-staffer-is-forced-out-over-a-controversial-
memo/535725/.

4. "The Changing Global Religious Landscape," Pew
Research Center, April 5, 2017, https://www.pewresearch.
org/religion/2017/04/05/the-changing-global-religious-
landscape/.

5. Nicole Kobie, "The Complicated Truth About China's
Social Credit System," *Wired*, July 6, 2019, https://www.
wired.co.uk/article/china-social-credit-system-explained.

CHAPTER 4

1. Wikipedia, s.v. "Toronto Blessing," accessed March 8, 2023,
https://en.wikipedia.org/wiki/Toronto_Blessing.

CHAPTER 5

1. Brittany Lee Allen, "When God Shakes His Church,"
Brittany Lee Allen (blog), accessed March 8, 2023, https://
brittleeallen.com/2016/10/when-god-shakes-his-church/.

2. Allen, "When God Shakes His Church."

CHAPTER 7

1. "Constitution of the United States: First Amendment,"
Constitution Annotated, accessed March 9, 2023, https://
constitution.congress.gov/constitution/amendment-1/.

2. Jess Blumberg, "A Brief History of the Salem Witch Trials,"
Smithsonian, updated October 24, 2022, https://www.
smithsonianmag.com/history/a-brief-history-of-the-salem-
witch-trials-175162489/.

3. "Extract from Thomas Jefferson's *Notes on the State
of Virginia*: Query XVII, 'Religion,'" Jefferson Quotes

and Family Letters, accessed March 9, 2023, https://tjrs.
monticello.org/letter/2260.

4. "Memorial and Remonstrance (1785)," Bill of Rights
Institute, accessed March 9, 2023, https://www.
billofrightsinstitute.org/primary-sources/memorial-and-
remonstrance.

5. Hana M. Ryman and J. Mark Alcorn, "Establishment
Clause (Separation of Church and State)," The First
Amendment Encyclopedia, accessed March 9, 2023, https://
www.mtsu.edu/first-amendment/article/885/establishment-
clause-separation-of-church-and-state.

6. Steven J. Heyman, "The Light of Nature: John Locke,
Natural Rights, and the Origins of American Religious
Liberty," Marquette University Law School, accessed March
9, 2023, https://scholarship.law.marquette.edu/mulr/vol101/
iss3/4/.

7. John R. Vile, "Masterpiece Cakeshop v. Colorado Civil
Rights Commission (2018)," The First Amendment
Encyclopedia, accessed March 9, 2023, https://www.mtsu.
edu/first-amendment/article/1596/masterpiece-cakeshop-v-
colorado-civil-rights-commission.

8. John R. Vile, "Fulton v. City of Philadelphia (2021)," The
First Amendment Encyclopedia, accessed March 9, 2023,
https://www.mtsu.edu/first-amendment/article/1916/fulton-
v-city-of-philadelphia.

9. "Stormans, Inc. v. Wiesman," Legal Information Institute,
accessed March 9, 2023, https://www.law.cornell.edu/
supremecourt/text/15-862.

10. John R. Vile, "Little Sisters of the Poor Saints Peter and
Paul, Home v. Pennsylvania (2020)," The First Amendment
Encyclopedia, accessed March 9, 2023, https://www.mtsu.
edu/first-amendment/article/1865/little-sisters-of-the-poor-
saints-peter-and-paul-home-v-pennsylvania.

11. Timothy S. Goeglein and Craig Osten, "Restoring Religious
Liberty: Why Freedom of Religion Does Not Mean

Freedom From Religion," *Touchstone*, October 18, 2019, http://www.touchstonemag.com/archives/addendum/restoring-religious-liberty.php.

CHAPTER 11

1. Franklin Sherman, "Dietrich Bonhoeffer: German Theologian," Britannica, updated January 31, 2023, https://www.britannica.com/biography/Dietrich-Bonhoeffer.
2. Sherman, "Dietrich Bonhoeffer."

AUTHOR'S NOTE

I F YOU HAVE enjoyed the message of this book, please join us at www.PastorTodd.org and become part of the remnant community. We have weekly online broadcasts that anyone from around the world can tune in to. God is moving in this remnant community, and we are in fact fulfilling the call to help develop an underground railroad for the remnant.

May the Lord bless you and keep you in Jesus' name!
—PASTOR TODD COCONATO